tim yearneau

He lives in Bloomington, Minnesota, a suburb of Minneapolis. He has always lived in this area, but has traveled everywhere. He plays a mean game of chess and takes on all comers on the ping pong table, and don't even talk about *Risk*. When the sun is shining and the sky is blue you might find him whipping around town on his bicycle. But when he is at home he tries to mimic Milo the dog and lounge about doing nothing, for both believe that sleep is not a waste of time. He does the Circuit at the health club and in between workouts you can find him downing moose tracks ice cream or a triple chocolate chunk cookie or just maybe some ribs from Mr. McCoy! His favorite fruit is pears and he eats oatmeal like there's no tomorrow for breakfast. Hey, he also has a Master's Degree from the University of St. Thomas.

follow tim on twitter
@timyearneau

www.timyearneau.com

www.facebook.com/mrybarbeque

www.youTube.com/yarndog50

ISBN-13: 978-1517234874

ISBN-10: 1517234875

Cover Design by
ebookLaunch.com

Senior-Editor-In-Chief
David Richmond Pearson

Curveballs

Sweet & Smokey Down the Barbeque Trail

a travelogue trilogy part i

Also by Tim Yearneau

Guide to Intellectual Property

Table of Contents

CHAPTER 1

in the beginning

As I sit here with my laptop at McDonald's in Dwight, Illinois, I hang head in shame. I tried to make it to I-57 BBQ in Chicago, but met defeat instead. Not by an enemy mind you, but by myself. Traffic jams, bad directions, lousy maps, late start, you name it. This was a rough beginning to what was supposed to be victory. I'm guessing I better tell you how I got here.

Many years ago I took career and personality tests. They came back with two recommendations: either become a priest or a rock 'n' roll musician. Perhaps a rock 'n' roll priest would be the best path. While the tests couldn't agree on the perfect career for me, they did agree on my personality—a keen, unrelenting sense of adventure. Travel feeds my curiosity like drugs feed an addict.

One philosophy of travel says there is only one way to get from Minneapolis to Los Angeles; i.e. the shortest distance between two points is a straight line. There are those whom I fought and argued with over this. That same philosophy holds that only the destination matters. *Bah.* I hold no such beliefs.

In that narrow view there is no space for the journey, the most important aspect. My ad hoc nature rejects terms like *linear* and *straight line*. They're foreign to my vocabulary. The best part of any trip is meeting a crossroads that leads to a sudden change of course, which turbocharges my inner explorer, thrusting me into a new direction. A map maker, charting one of my trips, would pause, scratch his head, take a sip of coffee, and then refuse to finish the map. I delight in knowing the agony I'd cause.

Most of us spend a great many waking hours pondering the great mysteries of life. We track down a route, slam into a roadblock, pursue another course, bump into an obstacle, make adjustments, and then continue on. In each path we search; we cannot, will not, rest.

Some chase important questions. Who will win the Superbowl? What's the purpose of life? Who am I? Who are my parents? Can cancer be cured? Can peace exist? Can a better mousetrap be built? I have chosen to stay more trivial. *Who* has the best barbeque? Be honest, at one time or another you've also wondered that, haven't you?

I find it necessary to mention that I work at a special education school district in the western suburbs of Minneapolis. What I do or where I work isn't of importance in my search for the perfect barbeque. Who I worked with is.

A good chunk of my job means sitting in the horseshoe shaped hallway where conversations run free and easy. Food, the glue that holds us together, flows like a river.

Sandifer and McCoy, two of my co-workers, grew up together. They eat and breathe sports. Saying they are highly competitive is an understatement. As basketball coaches they take no prisoners. Same for barbeque.

"My dad owned a rib place for four years. Did you know that?" Sandifer asked.

"No I did not," I said.

"I know how to make ribs."

"Who has better ribs? You or McCoy?"

McCoy couldn't hold back, "Forget about him. His don't compare to mine, sir. I make them Texas style, the right way, the McCoy way." For an unknown reason we refer to each other as sir. Nobody's figured out why or takes ownership for starting it.

Sandifer said, "Don't listen to him. His doesn't stand a chance against mine. He uses Open Pit in his sauce. Open Pit? Come on," followed by a hearty belly laugh.

"He doesn't even make them himself. It's his family's recipe. His uncle down in Arkansas makes them," McCoy responded, striking a condescending blow.

"You know, I want to try your ribs," I said, begging. "When do I get to try them? When?"

"I'm going to make a slab at home and bring in some for you," McCoy said.

"I'll have a football party at my place and you can come over," Sandifer said.

"Will you have ribs?"

"Sir, I'll make a slab just for you."

The competition was on. The debates, the bragging, and the arguments lasted for days, weeks, and months. Like a virus it spread to the whole building.

In their egotistical minds my co-workers failed to understand how a competitor could stand even a remote chance against them. "Theirs ain't nothing. Wait until you taste mine, it's nothing like you have ever tasted before. I make a special sauce with my secret ingredients that puts them to shame. I won *abc* contest and I won *xyz* contest and I won ...." A certain smugness always accompanied such words.

They stepped up the ferocity of their attacks. Each attempted to give the other a barbeque version of the figure four leg lock. Showing mercy never appeared to be an option.

Another question ping-ponged throughout my mind, "*Which* place has the best barbeque?" Asking it had the same effect as pouring gas on a fire.

"You think Big Daddy's is good? They're nasty. If you want the best, go to I-57 in Chicago."

"Big Jacks in Dallas. They do it right, Texas style."

"Are you looking for restaurants only? Or any place like a shack or trailer?"

"Any place."

"Try Interstate in Memphis. The others can talk all they want, but there is only one thing to say—Interstate."

"Salt Lick in Austin, man they rule."

"Mmmm ... Gates in Kansas City."

It would take a pallet full of paper to keep track of all the places they named. But the seeds were planted. The blood in my brain started circulating a bit faster, and the brainstorming began.

Were they full of it? Or dead on? Their strong opinions, impossible to ignore, couldn't be taken as fact. I burned with desire to know how their places stacked up to mine. Curiosity was killing the cat.

I had visions of making a Grand Loop heading south from Minneapolis, a place where ketchup is considered spicy, down to New Orleans via Kansas City and St. Louis, cruising through Mississippi and Alabama over to Florida, then up through Georgia, Tennessee, Kentucky, and Illinois before heading home.

I had traveled in summers past. Although each trip would start out with a definite plan, they would change as the trek progressed. For example, years ago I saw the Mission at San Juan Bautista while visiting the wine country of Napa Valley, adding an unplanned historical touch to a wine tasting excursion.

In another case, while attending a national rights festival in Washington D.C., an Orioles-Twins baseball game at Baltimore's Camden Yards found its spontaneous way into the itinerary.

Another time, on a trip out west to sell Australian hats, I detoured from the rigors of business by enjoying a bag lunch while sitting at the headwaters of the Missouri River. My current excursion would be no different. The theme is barbeque, yes, but I warn you, small bearable diversions will occur.

Checking my bank balance, reality set in. I had a week between the end of the regular school year and the beginning of summer school, with a Mantoux test in between. This placed debilitating limits. A five-day journey starting on that Wednesday and returning the following Sunday night was doable, but pushing it. Summer school started Monday morning, 8 am sharp.

* * *

I didn't wake up one day and say, "Oh, I should go in search for the perfect barbeque." Instead, a series of events over time led me in that direction. If you've never heard of the Chaos Theory, you have now.

It began innocently enough over a decade ago in downtown St. Paul, Minnesota. Old Kentucky BBQ opened up nearby, close to the offices of my employer, my older brother Pete. Unable to resist neither their lunchtime specials nor the aroma emanating from the place, I'd head over there more often than I care to admit. The taste of those ribs and the sides were off the charts. For a fact: they were to die for.

But Old Kentucky encountered financial difficulties and started skimping on sides, eventually closing. Sides, in my opinion, make or break the rib eating experience. I ask you, what would chocolate chip ice cream be without chocolate chips?

A couple of years later I worked at a Juvenile correctional facility. At lunch one day I blurted out, "Old Kentucky BBQ had the best ribs ever! Big Daddy owned it, and he was the best! But they closed. That sucks!" I made no attempt to hide my frustration.

The Chaplain heard me, stopped what he was doing, and looked up. Turning directly at me he said, "Big Daddy? I know him. We're related by marriage." I couldn't believe my ears. "He got his start setting up a smoker in Cub Foods parking lots on weekends. He went bankrupt after Old Kentucky BBQ, and had some serious health troubles."

This was distressing to me, but visions of those ribs never went away. A year later, as fate would have it, I received a phone call out of the blue from my friend Tami the Trucker. "Check out the news on TV. They had a feature on a guy who opened up a new barbeque place in St. Paul. Is this the guy you've been talking about?"

I rushed to the internet and researched it. Big Daddy's BBQ was back! I made urgent phone calls to Pete and Greg, my brothers. I forced them to drop everything and we cruised over there on a top priority mission.

I found Big Daddy sitting in a chair flush up against the back wall and introduced myself, relaying my conversation with the Chaplain. We yakked about it all: ribs, Old Kentucky BBQ, the new Big Daddy's, and he filled me in on his connection to the Chaplain.

I ordered my customary half-slab and dug in. Upon the first bite the world stopped. Glory had returned like MacArthur re-taking the Philippines. His ribs, sweet, smokey, and molasses-like, were the Gold Standard, destroying all comers. But not for long. I say this with a heavy heart.

The following summer I traveled to Ohio-Kentucky where I biked parts of the Underground Railroad Bike Trail, a 2200 mile route that stretches from Alabama to Canada; riding parts of it from Cincinnati, Ohio, to Louisville, Kentucky.

One sunny afternoon, driving along SR 122 near Batavia, Ohio, on the way to a trail point, a yellow oversized banner screamed barbeque. I followed the frontage road in my shiny new Ford Focus, rolling up to a big tent next to a BBQ trailer. There's something deliciously biting about discovering a new barbeque place sitting suspiciously by the side of the road. It's like when you ride a haunted trail on Halloween and all of a sudden a creature emerges from the bushes and screams "BOO!" It's what you came for.

Ever curious I asked Mike, the owner, "What's the secret to making great ribs?"

Well-built, wearing a skin-tight gray t-shirt and jeans, he loomed over me like a military man. Even his mustache had trim military protocol. Mike spoke with a don't-mess-with-me pride, peering at me with steely eyes. "It's all in the wood. I use Apple and take special trips up to Michigan and down to Georgia in my pickup to get it. Making barbeque is an art, not a science. Everyone has their own special way of making them."

I persisted. "How did you come to owning this barbeque trailer?"

His voice rose, "I was a salesman for 25 years, but recently got laid off. At 58 years old, I wasn't going to sit around and let anybody take care of me. I dug into my savings and bought this trailer. The owner of this storage facility was a client of mine and said I could set up here for free."

His body tightened and he leaned forward. "How is this economy going to come back? How are we going to make it?" Mike's voice trembled from the effects of the recession. "The next county over is so poor they have to use workers and services from our county to survive. The Ford plant down the road laid off 1800 people. How are they going to get those jobs back?"

For a brief moment in time I played his counselor, "I got whacked too. Fortunately, I still have a job. It doesn't pay as much as my previous one, but I still have a job. When the auto manufactures build better cars, buyers will come. That is how those jobs will come back." In hindsight, I'm not so sure I was all that reassuring.

It's a fate of irony that the intersection of a poor economy and a mutual love of barbeque caused us to meet on that sunny afternoon. His ribs were great, and his story gripping. Barbeque opened his heart and laid bare his inner psyche. I couldn't ask for more.

After gorging on Mike's barbeque, the motivation to get to Louisville increased like the decibel level at a Rolling Stones concert. I harbored a long, burning desire to visit Louisville. I didn't know much about it, but that didn't matter. It's where Muhammad Ali, *The Greatest of all Time*, grew up and that alone was reason enough.

He boxed in his prime during my youth and was my Idol. In fourth grade I wrote a poem about him for a class assignment: *Float like a Butterfly, Sting like a Bee*. I also knew he built the Muhammad Ali Museum in downtown Louisville. I wasn't about to miss it.

Louisville is also where Lewis and Clark formed their Corp of Discovery at the Falls of the Ohio. From there they embarked on one of the great adventures in American History, the Lewis and Clark Expedition. And I couldn't forget Louisville is home to Churchill Downs and the world famous Kentucky Derby.

Once in Louisville Pete reminded me, if not scolded me, that Kentucky is the center of barbeque country, "You're in Kentucky. You can't go there and not have ribs! You're in the center of it all. You have to try some. You'll regret it if you don't. Kentucky *is* barbeque. Go find some place. Go have some tonight. Call me back when you do."

He got me motivated. After researching the internet like a madman for the best barbeque ribs in Louisville, a couple of places rose to the surface. With an abundance of soul searching, Mark's Feed Store, a family-owned chain of five restaurants, won out. Their customer reviews swayed me.

Mark's Feed Store was the bomb! Baby back ribs. That pork slid right off the bone, causing us mere mortals to drop to our knees begging for more. Something about that sauce struck a nerve: sweet, like an irresistible nectar. Dang the Torpedoes. Their ribs possessed a light smokey barbeque tinge, suffocating the taste buds with a lifetime of flavor. The sides leaped off the plate, joining the armada of sensual delight.

I tried to deny it. I didn't want to admit it. I didn't want to say it. But Mark's Feed Store in Louisville, Kentucky, home of Muhammad Ali, owned the best barbeque ribs on the planet. Guilt and shame reigned supreme, being collateral damage from my Catholic upbringing. I had to confess they were a photo finish better than Big Daddy's. They were the new Gold Standard. The unfortunate truth was that The King had been replaced. (Sorry Mike, they got a slight nod over your ribs as well.)

* * *

You know that friend we all have, the one who hounds us with relentless persistence until we can take no more? In my case I've known Lisa Ocone for almost fifteen years. She hates losing in chess and refuses to go down with grace in a game of Risk. I've taken her on in the far corners of the globe, places like Uzbekistan, Poland, Austria, and Indonesia.

"You're good at writing, you should write a book about your travels," she said. "This guy wrote one about walking the Appalachian Trail and it ended up on the *New York Times* Best Seller List."

I constructed a wall of feeble resistance, but she blew right through it, pressing her attack with vigor and vive— something she has done to me on the chess board a hundred times. I asked her the name of the book, but she couldn't remember. She researched it and reported back it was *A Walk in the Woods* by Bill Bryson.

I had never heard of Bill Bryson before or of the

book she was referring to. So I went and picked up a copy and started reading it. The more I read it the more it tapped into my own sense of adventure, and triggered memories of the many trips I've taken. I continued to resist, however, and pooh-poohed the idea as gibberish.

But Lisa Ocone is very persistent and very persuasive. She kept after me. Soon I began to rationalize that if Bill Bryson can write a travelogue book about walking the Appalachian Trail and hit it big, why not me? Before I knew it, I gave in. Jealousy and greed are good bedfellows.

* * *

Another battle ensued between me and those linear people; my editors in particular. A mere split-second from tipping over their coffee mugs and smashing them, I said to them, "Oh, so you think I should just show up at the front door of a barbeque place in Chicago, write about it, and then miraculously show up at the front door of a barbeque place in St. Louis, write about it, and so on and so on?"

"Yes," they said with a straight face.

"No! I'm *not* writing a barbeque restaurant review book. I'm writing a travelogue with a barbeque theme. There's a difference. The stuff in-between is the meat and potatoes. Why is that so hard to understand?"

They huffed and puffed and threatened to blow the door down. Good for them. But in the end, I won the argument. *Hah*! And BTW, I wouldn't have cleaned up the mess either.

CHAPTER 2

unbelievable, unbelievable

I gave much thought to where I would first eat barbeque on my tour. This was a big decision for me. Based on my conversations with co-workers and friends I had a very specific list of barbeque establishments I wanted to visit. But I didn't want to cheat myself by skipping a place I might come across at random. Variety is the spice of life, and I wasn't about to end up on the short end of that stick.

I mulled over options until my brain hurt, and played scenarios over and over in my mind until I got sick of them. Finally, I made a decision. I-57 BBQ in Chicago would be my inaugural stop. Until then, nada, no barbeque. This decision made it easy to designate the day as a purely travel day.

Once I get on the road, I can get away with flying by the seat of my pants like a rock star, but it's an Achilles heel now where planning is required. I needed to drive from Minneapolis to a campground 60 miles outside of Chicago. Certainly this was doable in a day.

But I had much to do to get ready, with the multitasker in me standing at the ready, like a foot soldier ready to follow orders. I had to pack, get my Mantoux reading, and get a tune-up for the car. The last item went down in flames, a victim of a time crunch. Two out of three wasn't bad.

"Make sure you give me the names, addresses and phone numbers of all the places you are staying, just in case," my dad said.

"I don't know where I'm staying yet. I haven't thought that far ahead," I said, not remembering the name of the campground.

"Then give me your cell phone number before you leave."

"Okay, I hope I remember to charge my cell phone. Have you seen the charger lying around?"

I had other things on my mind, too, like hockey. It didn't matter I was embarking on a barbeque tour, the Stanley Cup Finals were in full swing. Hockey is the best of all the major sports rolled into one high-flying game. I was born and raised in Minnesota, so it makes sense we're all possessed by hockey, like Texas is by football or Brazil is by soccer. We're known as the State of Hockey for a reason.

I concerned myself mightily with finding a place to watch the game. I needed to get to that campground at a reasonable hour, but watching the game was of utmost importance. I didn't want to be too far away, for the game might not end until quite late, and I didn't want to have to drive much during the wee hours. And who knows, once the game was over I might get motivated and go have some mad fun in downtown Chicago.

Regardless, I got the Mantoux reading late morning and started driving. I sailed down the road without a care in the world. Visions of savory ribs slathered in the most scintillating sauces imaginable left me drooling.

But Mother Nature wasn't so kind. She decided to curse me by showering down an avalanche of rain, rain, and more rain, slowing my progress. Other fools ignorant enough to travel came to the same fate. A turtle moved faster.

Small bouts of panic attacks sprouted as 7 pm approached, the start time of the game. I stomped on the accelerator and, admittedly, stretched the speed limit a teeny-weeny bit.

The clock on the dashboard delivered nagging

reminders about the hour at hand. In Oconomowoc, 25 miles before Milwaukee, Rosati's Pizza had all the elements of a robust man-cave: booths to the side, a straight on view of the TV, and a menu with eye popping options. I stuck to my guns and stayed with my decision to not eat barbeque. Spaghetti and meatballs would have to do.

Speaking of barbeque, I have a confession to make: when I order barbeque I'm not real daring. I always order the half-slab ribs. I can't help myself. I know there are other great barbeque things to order; hot links, pulled pork, pork butts, catfish, brisket, chicken wings, sausage, ham, whatever. So I have to come clean; when I say I'm in search for the perfect barbeque—*translated*—that means I'm in search for the perfect ribs. I just stay in my lane. Yummy!

Anyways, I got myself situated in a booth at Rosati's and ordered. A good book waited in silence in my backpack, daring me to open it and turn its pages. It was *Churchill,* by Paul Johnson. I had bought it just before leaving as a way to kill time. The problem with a good book, especially a biography, is that I can't put the dang thing down. I indulged myself and ate as I read.

One final piece of the puzzle remained. "Would you mind turning to the hockey game? It's game seven of the Stanley Cup Finals. It's really big," I said to the waitress.

"Not a problem," she said.

"Would you turn up the sound, too?"

"Sure."

Not to brag, but I'm a skilled multitasker; few are as adept at the art. Oh, I'm that good. I fired on all eight cylinders. I sat there in my man-cave and went to it; a bite of spaghetti here, read a few pages there, watch some bruising body-checks, chow down some meatballs, flip through a few more pages, cheer a soaring slap-shot, and so on and so forth. I had it grooving, boy.

The spaghetti and meatballs were to die for. It

pleased my palate like a feather tickles the skin. A quiet focus I hadn't experienced all day led to a state of restorative serenity. Time slipped away ... and I bothered no one.

Doggonit, without warning the peace vanished. A short fat guy emerged from the shadows and abruptly changed the channel to a Milwaukee Brewers baseball game. *Jerk!* This was uncalled for. Who would do such a thing? *Fat Boy!*

I was pissed, and readied myself to give him a piece of my mind. I really wanted to slug him in the gut, but that would go against every value my dad instilled in me.

Instead, I scanned for allies. But I didn't find any. All of them were baseball fans who could care less about Game 7 of the Stanley Cup Finals. *Losers!*

I held my tongue and ceded ground, moving in full retreat. I scrambled to the door and made a swift, decisive exit to the car. I slammed the key in the ignition, stomped on the accelerator, and peeled out of there; all the while hurling defecating words in their direction, with not an ounce of mercy in my soul.

* * *

Those darn stinking tollways. I hate them. They are time-consuming and expensive. *Sigh.* Regardless, they are an unmovable fact of life when driving to Chicago. The smooth efficient traveler is slowed down by them at such an alarming rate the authorities might as well put down spike strips.

At 11:30 pm on that clear night, a certain dullness overwhelmed the roadway—wide open, clean and modern—leading to the first toll. Road signage, attached to metal horseshoe bars, extended over the freeway, similar in construction to newly built freeways. A fluorescent brown haze dimly lit the air. Having driven on Chicago tollways many times before, they always seemed like ancient ruins. The modern feel of this roadway felt strange.

I fumbled with the pop and camera, doing everything an idiot would do. I had to stay awake somehow. Grandiose visions of making viral YouTube videos fired my imagination. I was distracted, but *not* texting.

Red and green lights glowed bright above the toll gate and, strange enough, soon appeared to the far right, instead of in front. I made a cursory check in my rear view mirror and noticed the glow of the red and green lights were now behind me.

I only thought the worst. Now in the iPass lane for people who prepay and use transponders, I convinced myself an army of police cars, lights strobing and spotlights glaring, would soon pull me over. Fear paralyzed me.

Thankfully, the nightmare of becoming a newspaper headline never materialized. Instead, a bare lonely sign informed me I could pay for my mistake online. While I did feel a certain amount of shame for bungling something so simple, I felt more a sense of relief than anything.

Tired and hungry though, I entertained thoughts of ignoring it and not paying them altogether in the slim hope the problem would disappear. I knew better. 20 years ago in Chicago I attempted to get away with a fast one. I got caught, effectively, with my hand in the cookie jar and it turned into a disaster of the highest proportions.

I confessed my moral failings to the worker manning the next toll. He handed me a pink form with the smirk of a Catholic priest, as though handing down a penance. The next day I erased the sins of my past with a single keystroke, transferring to the City of Chicago the entire sum of $1.50.

* * *

Right before exiting for the Lake Forest Oasis, the interstate sign said *Chicago 30 miles.* Something was wrong. The Oasis that led to the campground should have been 60 miles from Chicago. First the debacle at Rosati's earlier in the evening, and now this. It was 12:45 am on a strange tollway with no map or known name of campground. Nothing felt right. Time to fill the gas tank.

The saving grace in debacles like these is that gas station attendants know everything, like engineers. Prepaying $35 for the gas, the actual cost came to $31. The attendants made grand attempts to refund the difference. They each took turns swiping my credit card. A puzzled look followed each swipe. I remained patient. They punched buttons on the keyboard with a fury, making phone calls to who knows who asking who knows what.

I went for it. I had to know. "Do you know if there are any campgrounds near here?"

The three attendants, an African woman, a white male Caucasian, and a Russian lady with a thick accent, all stared at me with blank looks. After a painful pause one of them answered, "No, there are no campgrounds near here."

My nightmare scenario had been confirmed; no campgrounds on I-94. Pouring salt on a wound would have felt better.

Columbia University in downtown Chicago used to be a youth hostel back in the day. I thought about staying there, but for reasons that seemed brilliant at the time, I dismissed it. This left only the dreaded nuclear option:

drive 30 more miles into downtown Chicago, get on I-90 north, and drive an additional 60 miles to the campground.

Desperate to avoid this fate, I decided to inquire at a motel. Entering, I asked, "Do you have a room available?"

"No I'm sorry, we don't."

At another motel I felt more optimistic, "Do you have a room available, and if so how much?"

"No, we're full for the night."

At each motel other desperate travelers inquired about a room as well, each leaving in despair after getting the same bad news. The fact that others were hunting for a room changed my search into a survival of the fittest.

Sprinting into the lobby of one motel, I conversed with a couple who was also on the prowl. They had the same story: the motels were packed full and rates were through the roof.

"Do you have any rooms available?" I asked the clerk.

"Yes, we have one room available." The competitor within me burned. It's 1:30 am, and I need this room more than they do, I thought. You have each other, no offense, but this one's mine. And besides, I'm the one on a barbeque tour.

Preparing to unleash the full arsenal, I asked the clerk, "How much does it cost for the night?" I had been willing to go up to $80.

"It's $200 for the night," she replied.

Are you crazy?

I stomped on the accelerator. My Ford Focus shot down the road like a race car on steroids. After covering nearly 100 miles of boring monotonous cement, I exited at the Des Plaines Oasis exit, confident I got it right this time.

I still had to find the campground though. I drove

and drove under dark blank skies, navigating a lone windy road past ominous farms in the dead of night.

I toyed with the idea of staying at a nearby KOA campground, but they had no obvious way to pay after close. The straw that broke the camel's back was the sign on their door. They now charged for four campers minimum per site because of higher gas prices. *Yeah right.*

I finally found the campground I was looking for. I recognized it from when I had stayed there a year earlier. Situated between a couple of straight country roads, the center of it was occupied by a long narrow open area. Stimulating gentle green languished everywhere, with generous amounts of breezy trees lining the outskirts.

I have lots of sympathy for those who operate campgrounds. Door knobs like me rob them of their sleep when we pick up the black phone on their office wall and buzz them at 3 am, begging pitifully for a campsite.

When I picked up the phone, instead of a soothing and understanding voice on the other end, a series of *beep, beep, beep* noises resonated through it. Tired and not willing to continue the fight, I picked a campsite at random, pitched my tent, and fell asleep.

CHAPTER 3

you've got to be kidding me

On this Thursday morning, sun rays roamed the rural sky leaving bounce and glee in their path. There is a mischievous appreciation for waking at 9 am, knowing that there are those who go out of their way to brag about the greatness of getting up at the crack of dawn.

Lying in the tent those conversations came to mind, recalling statements like, "You don't know what you are missing," and, "Oh, I get so much done at that time of day." They proceed to list all of their accomplishments before I even open my eyes. Their attempts at superiority fall on deaf ears.

Needing all the energy I could muster, today, my search for the perfect barbeque would begin in earnest. Not a soul stirred, except for a slow moving elderly man walking his dog. Agenda items overflowed: bike around downtown Chicago, make an inquiry at the Library, buy a Father's Day present for my dad at the Hershey's Store, eat ribs at I-57, and drive towards St. Louis.

A new truth abounded, stunning me, and all who come to find it. Campgrounds cater to the RV crowd with their big 35 foot puffers, providing them with convenient hook ups for water and electricity. The rest of us who pitch tents are an afterthought. A true camper aspires to be one with nature; electricity and running water defeat that vision. And on top of all that, it cost me a mind-blowing $36 for the campsite. Yes, I know I'm ranting, but I *have* to get it out of my system.

I experienced serious cravings for oatmeal at

McDonald's, as eating ribs would be my last act of the day, not the first. But after taking a shower, packing the tent, and heading down the road, a moment of weakness occurred. I skipped McDonald's and instead pulled into a simple-looking restaurant.

The stern white rambler of a building was adorned with a black piercing roof. The inside offered nothing spectacular. It looked like a typical family restaurant with brown booths and brown tables. A bare heartbeat of life existed even though peak breakfast time was at hand. The waitress, a woman in her late thirties, maybe early forties, came and took my order—a ham and cheese omelet with hash browns.

I'm not very good at managing time. In fact, I'm terrible at it. I flipped through the pages of *Churchill* at a steady clip and before you know it, *poof*, there went the time. While eating, my belly experienced a disagreeable sense of dissatisfaction. The hash browns were not golden brown as I expected. Instead they were a greasy conglomeration of potatoes glued together by the grease itself. The omelet displayed a burnt brownish muddiness that made it unappetizing.

I made an instant decision to slip money under the napkin and slink out of the booth. I prayed the waitress wouldn't catch me and ask if I had liked the food. This would lead to a moral dilemma; do I spit out the truth or tell a white lie? The omelet and hash browns were bad! Being a chronic people pleaser, it pains me to deliver bad news.

I moved with urgency and in my good fortune the waitress didn't spot me. *Whew.* I cruised down the windy road to my original choice, McDonald's. They have the best mocha frappe on the planet. FYI, the coffee taste isn't even real coffee, it's just a flavored syrup.

I flipped through page after page of *Churchill*, hooked like an addict. In between pages I slurped sips, alternating between the Diet Coke and frappe. Something earth shattering happened there—at least earth-shattering to me.

I made an unexpected and surprising discovery researching the internet for the best way to get from Chicago to St. Louis. I wanted to get up and yell from the highest mountain top. But I didn't want to make a scene so I kept it to myself and celebrated with internal explosions.

There it was, the miracle of a lifetime! Route 66. *The Mother Road.* The Alpha and the Omega. The Beginning and the End. I'd dreamed of driving on it since high school. And now it looked to be a storming possibility. My morning shifted into overdrive. All of a sudden I had life and buzz.

The Mother Road starts at the intersection of Jackson Street and Lake Shore Drive in Chicago. But soon my dream turned to doubt. Over time the original Route 66 had fallen into a rundown state like an old broken-down car. A small possibility existed of driving on its remnants all the way to St. Louis, where a plate or two of ribs awaited me with open arms. But was it feasible?

I found a possible solution. Highway 55 ran parallel to Route 66. But something rubbed me the wrong way about this. Driving on it would feel like a fraud, like buying a fake Rolex watch rather than buying the original. The dream was to drive on the original Route 66, not a freeway running parallel to it. Learning that every exit on highway 55 connected to the original Route 66 or close to it, re-ignited my spirits; it was an agreeable, bearable, compromise.

The time had come to leave. The beauty of the day radiated everywhere. But upon entering the freeway, my car came to a sudden halt. So did every other vehicle. Thinking a mistake had occurred, I looked in all directions, but no one moved. When I say no one moved

I don't mean they moved at a slow crawl. It's as though each car had super glue applied to their tires.

My dream of eating ribs at I-57 BBQ halted too. What time did they close? 9 pm? Road rage bubbled to the surface. Fumigating, I burned to yell out the window, "You no good rotten bums! Get moving! You jerks! Move it!" I placed all blame on the other motorists' shoulders.

Weighing my options, I soon got out of denial and surrendered to the situation. I didn't want to, but accepted it. I stayed in my lane, rolled up the windows, turned on the air conditioner, and tuned in to a good radio station.

I tried to figure out a great way to kill time while sitting there, moving at the speed of zero. After a whirlwind brainstorming session, it became my mission to make observations:

There are red cars, green cars, blue cars, black cars, multi-colored cars, and just about any color you could dream of. Two-wheel drive, four-wheel drive, and all-wheel drive. All shapes and sizes. Small, medium, large, extra large, double extra large, triple extra large, and so large there is no name for them. Some vehicles are high off the ground, while some are low to the ground. New vehicles, old vehicles, and everything in between.

Motorcycles are the noisiest with their deafening puh, puh, puh, and that is when they are idling. Some vehicles have fancy paint jobs and lots of shiny chrome. Others are rust buckets, dull, and ugly. Gas-powered, diesel-powered, green-powered, and electric-powered. I didn't see solar-powered though.

Oodles of Japanese brands, American brands, European brands, and Korean brands. Some have fancy spinner rims while others are lucky just to have their wheels still rolling.

Tires are made by the likes of Goodyear, Michelin, Firestone, Bridgestone, Hankook, and brands I'd never heard of. I realized there are a lot of people driving on some very bald tires. Shame on them.

The pickup truck with high wooden sides in the back bed took the Grand Prize. It held what looked like an entire lifetime of possessions. Stuff stuck out in all directions.

My observations were proof I had too much time on my hands. In the end, navigating the minefield of stationary vehicles took 3 long drawn-out hours. Exhausting. They say there are only two things in life that are certain, death and taxes. But there is a third. The reason for traffic not moving: road construction in Chicago.

But later, a paranormal phenomenon occurred that I struggled to explain. The closer I approached the tolls, the faster traffic moved. But it couldn't be! I say this because at these very same tolls are completely stopped vehicles. They have to be completely stopped in order to pay their fee. It is a scientific and legal fact, they *must* stop.

I questioned how traffic could speed up near a toll when traffic at the toll itself is stopped. Applying scientific reasoning, my car would have to slow down approaching a toll booth to not bash into a slowing-down vehicle in front of me who doesn't want to bash into a completely stopped vehicle ahead of them.

But the closer I approached the toll the more my speedometer needle moved to the right. Engine noise increased; RPMs jetted. My whole car tilted with every acceleration. Objects in the rear view mirror got smaller. With each sideways turn of my head a different vehicle appeared. I'm not versed in the science of traffic flow near tolls, but it happened. I sped up. *I know, I know ....*

* * *

I arrived in downtown at 3:45 pm and in a time crunch. To alleviate this problem the multitasker within crafted a brilliant solution. Cut nothing, but spend less time doing each thing. I unloaded my bike, strapped on the flag helmet, paid the attendant, and shot from the parking lot like a cannonball. I had those pedals spinning. Cars and trucks and busses zoomed close, weaving in and out of their lanes. Every now and then the world shook from the gusts of a passing semi.

Mixed in with the nervous *whoosh, whoosh, whoosh* of the cars and the angry *roar, roar, roar* of the trucks I heard an awful lot of *honk, honk, honk*. I came to the singular conclusion honking is a time-honored Chicago tradition.

I made grand efforts to bob and weave to avoid being crushed by the armada of moving steel that was mere inches away. I scraped a lot of curbs. I bounced up and down them, too. I still made like a gazelle though. I made a sharp turn right at the next set of lights and darted the final few blocks to Michigan Avenue.

I sprinted up the steps to the first big building and rushed through the doors, the air filled with lofty expectations. Soon, however, my expectations dropped like the Dow.

Reading 4:30 pm on the wall clock, I asked the clerk, "Is there a library near here?" speaking in short, rapid bursts with sweat dripping down, and flinging my hands in ninja like movements.

The clerk smiled and with pleasant calm directed me to go down the street straight out from the building, take a left on State Street, and head over to Van Buren where I would find the library.

I did so and seemingly pedaled forever. Flummoxed, I stopped and asked a traffic cop, "Do you know where the public library is? I was told it was on State Street."

Sticking her arm out, she said, "Go down that street, take a left to State, then go right." Her grim face spit the words abruptly. She wasted no time in turning her back on me, continuing to direct traffic. She seemed to hate my guts.

Following her directions as best as any human could, self-doubt creeped in. I stopped again and asked a woman walking along the sidewalk for directions. She smiled and pointed to a building. In a soft, bubbly tone she said, "You are real close, just continue down this street past that tall black building. Take a right on the next street, which is State. Bike a little bit and you will see it." She took her time, making sure I understood what building she was referring to.

"Thank you," I said, full of gratitude.

After riding past the tall black building, State Street still did not show itself. Are people lying to me, I thought, or am I a moron?

Approaching another traffic cop I asked, "Do you know where the public library is? I was told it was on State Street."

Taking a page from the first traffic cop, he turned and glared. He pointed to a building behind me, and said, "There it is." No warm fuzzies. No smiles. Nothing. He also wasted no time in turning his back on me, continuing to direct traffic. He seemed to hate my guts, too.

Turning around, there it was. I locked the bike to the street pole and marched in to the first information booth in sight, ready to conduct business. I asked the clerk, "Do you carry eBooks in this library and who would I speak to about getting my business book carried here?" The sweat moving down my forehead went from a trickle to something bigger. My words hit the floor in rapid succession, and my hands still moved like a ninja.

"Yes we do," he said. "Let me give you the name of our media specialist who handles this." He opened the desk drawer nice and slow, pulling out the proper business card. He paused and then smiled at me saying, "Here you go."

Could you be any slower, I thought, snapping the card from his hand.

The time for I-57 BBQ loomed on the radar. But doubts crept in. *How often am I in Chicago? When will I ever visit this Library again? Can't the ribs wait a little longer? Screw it.*

My first darts down the hallways began. One floor, then another, then another, discovering all that an avid lover of books could, like Jacques Cousteau exploring ocean depths for new discoveries. Closing time inched closer and closer. Up escalators and down escalators. Up flights of stairs, then down flights of stairs, always at the same manic clip.

They had old and new collections covering everything from the beginning of mankind to the digital age. Multi-media exhibits of all kinds dotted the building. Those were the best. Short movies and long ones too. For kids, teens, and adults. Stay and watch it now or rent a DVD and view it at home. Endless possibilities stretched and pulled the imagination. I raced from rack to rack like an Olympic athlete. New discoveries competed with each other for my attention. Small books, regular sized books, and oversized books on subjects that blew my mind like gargoyles, Zen, and Hindu gods. Did you know a Hindu god agreed to settle a score with his enemy over a game of chess, and then cheated during the game? Yep, it's true.

Locating the restroom shared the same degree of difficulty as pulling teeth. The security guard, looking above my head into the spacial distance said, "Go up the escalator, down around the hallway, turn right at the end." His stoic body didn't flinch an inch and he wouldn't look at me. Despite his crummy directions, I found it.

The computer lab on one of the upper floors contained row upon row of computers, a virtual army of black monotonic machines. The entire listless array of them were in use; pity the poor fellow who hoped to get on one.

An odd sensation overcame me. All of the computer users were calm. No sweat, no speaking in rapid-fire, no darting around, no hand motions. Calm. Lifeless. Why weren't they surfing the internet with a final fury or sending their last emails with abandon? Didn't they know that the library was closing and that they would be shooed away by security guards in a matter of minutes? They continued on without a care in the world. Strange indeed.

The main hallway contained an appealing black and white photography exhibit. A citizen had made a hobby of creating a historical timeline of Chicago in pictures. Rushing from picture to picture absorbing the history shared in each photograph, time slipped away.

Convinced closing time was upon me, I scurried outside into the welcoming sunshine, taking note of the writing on the door. Once outside it dawned on me why the users in the lab were calm and lifeless. The library didn't close until 9 pm. Only on weekends did they close early. Oh shoot.

It would have been easy to stop crossing off agenda items and head straight to I-57 to eat ribs. Nope. My stubborn joined with the optimist. I liked the freedom and exhilaration of biking in downtown Chicago too much, refusing to give that up for the sake of getting barbeque a little early.

Biking free and easy, pedaling at a steady clip, the calories burned away like a fog in the sun. An abundance of shops, restaurants, bars, and clubs lined both sides of Rush Street. The air filled with the aroma of Italian eateries.

Motorists on that stretch of pavement gave no regard for bicyclists. Cars and trucks and buses cruised with abandon. At certain intervals the gap between my bicycle tires and the curb got smaller and smaller to the point I started curb scraping, forcing me into a complete stop.

In each instance I dismounted and stood on the pavement, contemplating a solution. Eventually, I swung my right foot up over the bike frame onto the high, cliff-like curb, leaving my left foot touching the pavement in the most minimal fashion, and causing me to tilt at a weird angle. By now the vertical clearance between my crotch and the bike frame amounted to zero. But in a final act of heroism I attempted to yank the entire bike frame high up onto the sidewalk. This only resulted in pain and failure.

A few well-placed curses for the Chicago City planners provided a token amount of emotional satisfaction. Effecting a complete dismount I manually lifted the entire bike up onto the sidewalk, remounted, and resumed pedaling. I reentered Rush Street a short distance later only to encounter more motorists with no regard for bicyclists. Then, the sad process repeated itself.

At long last, the desired cross street appeared and I made a glorious right turn, destined for the Hershey's Store. Stopping for tea along the way delivered a nice breather from the trauma of biking that treacherous road.

The Hershey's Store sits right behind the famous Water Tower on the north end of Michigan Avenue, a block from the John Hancock Center. Wanting to buy my dad a Father's Day present there ever since my last visit a year ago, it was the last obstacle between me and my goal of I-57 BBQ.

Ahh, the Hershey's Store. One's senses soar strolling through the aisles. Everything is inviting. The ambience. The colors. The chocolates. The smells. The souvenirs. It becomes impossible to leave. The clock on the wall foretold an impending time crunch. I couldn't let the chocolates at the Hershey's Store stand in my way. It was time to go.

One of the great pleasures of Chicago is the never-ending flow of energy. There is no other singular rewarding experience similar to bicycling down Michigan Avenue, absorbing the pulse of the city as it goes about its daily routine. On every block there exist shops for every purpose and taste. Jutted buildings soar toward the clouds emitting long happy shadows. Every corner provides opportunities to observe the beauty of the human race in action. Young, old, male, female, black, white, big, small, walking, biking, sitting, standing, eating, laughing, serious, fast, slow, rich, poor. The pulse, the energy, the electricity created there exists nowhere else.

The path back to the car rolled by Millennium Park, a vast overreaching park containing statues, shops, art, walking paths, and events. The crown jewel of Chicago, it sits right next to Lake Michigan.

Approaching the park the drumbeat of rock 'n' roll vibrated in the air. The crowd reflected a microcosm of culture with the added spice of hippies, tattoos, nose rings, and those new fangled ear loops. They ate hot dogs, drank beer, smiled, cheered, and whooped with every note. Spurred on, the Generation-X band let loose, ionizing the atmosphere into atomic frenzy.

Each band member's hairstyle had the look of someone who'd just rolled out of bed with hair sticking in all directions and in need of a good shampoo. Their dark clothes weren't much different: wrinkled and crinkled like the skin of a really old man. This must be the chic look of the modern band, I thought.

They played with a rhythmic beat, like the *bang, bang, bang* made when pots are hit against each other in repeated fashion. Every song had the same groove. I had no cares, moving back and forth, left and right like everyone else.

* * *

I-57 BBQ is a family owned chain that started with one store on 115th Avenue in south Chicago. Based on a map pulled up from the internet, I decided to go to a closer one on the 6500 block of Western Avenue. This would be the inaugural barbeque stop on the Mr. Y. BBQ Tour, the last event in an otherwise uneventful day. I had soaring expectations. All the thinking. All the plotting. All the planning. The journey to get here. It all came down to this.

I exited the parking lot and stepped on the gas, heading for I-90 north. The car clock read 8 pm. It couldn't be far away, I thought, and even if they closed at 9 pm there was plenty of time. Traffic jams, I rationalized, would cease to exist when the sun went down. I figured cross streets would be marked very clearly and I'd find the 6500 block with ease, so easy it'd be like stealing candy from a baby.

I'm so stupid. Traffic jams in Chicago don't stop because the sun goes down. Chicago is a city that never sleeps. Traffic jams only pick up in pace. I defined the moron in oxymoron.

Furthermore, the street signs on the bridges would say something like 2800, which I interpreted to mean the 2800 block. Using linear, straight-line logic (something I hate to begin with), I anticipated seeing 6500 on a bridge coming to me soon. It didn't work that way. The street planners that designed Chicago must have crossed paths in another life with the street planners that designed Eden Prairie, Minnesota.

My car clocked flipped from 8 pm to 8:15 pm to 8:30 pm to 9 pm to 9:30 pm to 9:45 pm, bringing me to the mysterious 7000 block of Harlem at 10 pm.

"How do I get to Western and 65th?" I asked the attendant at a gas station there.

"I'm sorry. I don't know."

Marching across the street to another gas station, I asked, "How do I get to Western and 65th?"

"I'm sorry. I don't know," the attendant there said.

A local assured me with an uneasiness that, "It's not close to here." I wrote him off as doubtful.

Another more confident local said, "Oh man, you are a long ways away."

"Am I sort of close?"

"Nope."

Venom and curses to the internet map. He rattled off something about the Dan Ryan Express and Highway 55 and all sorts of funk. Listening to those directions as best I could, I nodded as though understanding, praying to remember them.

Not trusting what I heard, I ended up on Western Avenue right off the Eisenhower Expressway. A new sense of danger lurked, so I stopped at a convenience store to ask for help.

As a human being, a mortal, I fall victim to judging others based on preconceived notions. Being in a questionable part of town and the only white person in a crowd of African-Americans, late at night, I let my fears and insecurities take over. I'm not saying that it's right; I could have used a priest to confess the sinful judgments I made about my fellow man.

I headed into the convenience store ready to bolt at a moment's notice. Timid and apprehensive, I asked those in front of me in line for directions. Silly me. They couldn't have been more helpful or friendly.

The shortest distance between two points is a straight line, and based on the directions, I headed straight down Western Avenue. I soon found myself heading into the heart of South Chicago, an area whose reputation for crime and violence would stop the bravest adventurer in his tracks.

Years ago, another traveler and I stopped in the heart of South Chicago on a sunny afternoon to look at a map, attempting to locate the University of Chicago. Upon telling this to a local he said we shouldn't have stopped at all, and if anyone stood in front of our car to run them over—it was that dangerous.

Rolling further south, memories of this past experience danced in my head. At an intersection a convoy of police cars blew by me at a furious speed, their red and blue lights flashing in the night sky. *This is crazy*. And so it is that at 11:30 pm on a warm clear evening I conceded defeat, a beaten warrior. There would be no barbeque at I-57.

Highway 55, the ticket to St. Louis, was a hop, skip, and a jump away. Lightning struck a third time as infinite road construction battled any progress. It took 30 minutes to move a foot stomping 3 miles. My nerves were shot and my patience worn razor thin. *Get me out of Chicago by any means, please.*

At 1:45 am, with bleary eyes, the building sitting alone and isolated by the frontage road looked like a typical low-budget motel. After ringing the bell a little Indian man appeared.

"How much?"

"I will charge you $40, including tax." He sounded more like a car salesman trying to close a deal with a rock bottom price that would blow his prospective customer away.

He put an overt emphasis on *$40*, raising his hands from his side to his chest, then slamming them outward attempting to create an arresting effect. He didn't need to sell it that hard, for my desperation and exhaustion dominated all else.

CHAPTER 4

success at last, success at last

Upon waking up Friday morning and scanning my motel room, it hit me why the low price. Even with the lights on, night vision goggles were needed to see anything—there were dim shadows everywhere. Faded paint and torn wallpaper covered the walls. The sheets, blankets, and pillows smelled like cigarettes. I'm not a smoker. I don't recall drinking water from a clean glass either. At least the towels were clean. Thank goodness I only needed a bed to sleep in, and that my eyes were closed the whole time.

The day started with a heavy dose of mental flogging. How could I screw this up so bad? What was I thinking? I spent all this time and effort to get to I-57 BBQ and missed it. Dummy.

The only way to let go of the nightmare of the night before was to score a major victory in Springfield, home of Honest Abe Lincoln. Plus, I vowed to return to Chicago at some point and eat at I-57. I had to turn lemons into lemonade.

The clerk's animated behavior the night before could easily be explained by the large Motel 6 sign right next to his business. Rooms there were $40, too; competition makes you better.

A McDonald's located next door unleashed my cravings for oatmeal. Adding WiFi to each and every one of their restaurants in the entire country was a stroke of genius that gave the wandering traveler a measure of comfort. One of my co-workers, commenting on his trip to Arizona said, "I could be driving through the middle of nowhere late at night, into some small Podunk town, and if it had a McDonald's, I knew I would have WiFi."

In this part of Illinois there isn't only a McDonald's in every major town, there is one every exit or two. The number of McDonald's per capita here is astonishingly high.

I did it again: lost track of time reading *Churchill*. By now it's a disease. *Tick, tock, tick, tock,* the hands on the clock zoomed around and around. Visions of writing a daily travelogue never materialized, due to my constant going to bed late, poor eating, and questionable sleep.

I narrowed barbeque in Springfield to two places, Popeye's and Corky's. The list shrank to one after learning Corky's was no longer in business. Calling Popeye's, an African-American owned business, a pleasant sounding voice on the other end provided simple directions and confirmed their operating hours.

Hanging up, a flash of brilliance struck. I should market my business book to the small town libraries I pass through along the way. They tend to be friendlier, and it's easier to get hold of the right person.

The business book I'm referring to is the ever informative *Guide to Intellectual Property*, authored by yours truly. Brilliantly written with simple lessons and excellent examples it has climbed the charts, listed as number 74 on a top 75 list for intellectual property on VeryWellSaid.com. No need to mention that, to date, my book has generated seven sales; one of them to dear old dad, and another to my sister's dog Milo.

The tiny but fun city of Dwight, 75 miles southwest of Chicago, loomed a few blocks down the road, which made my marketing campaign all the more brilliant. Entering Dwight required driving on a dull grayish two lane country road. I headed straight a short distance, took a sharp jog right, and then continued through alternating fields of bush, grass, and trees.

Catching a glance of a street sign, I screeched,

"Whooooey, yeeehhaaah, yipppeeee!" My curious reason for joy lay in the letters and numbers on the sign: OLD RTE 66. *"Hah, ha. I'm on it. I'm on the original Route 66. I'm on Rooooot 66!"* I bounced up and down on the car seat in a victory dance. I shot my hands skyward. I drooled. I dribbled. I lost all sense of control. I never smiled bigger.

A short distance past the WELCOME TO DWIGHT sign, another glimmer caught my eye. Looking to the right, my jaw dropped, and my foot slammed on the brakes. My car lurched forward, then bobbed backwards as it stopped with sudden force. Staring motionless, paralyzed ... *"Whooooey, yeeehhaaah, yipppeeee!"* Another victory dance in the car seat. My hands shot skyward again. I drooled. I dribbled. I lost all sense of control; peeling into the small driveway and not caring that part of my car stuck out into the street.

Sitting there was a colorful structure, like a Thomas Kinkade painting, of two small squarish buildings joined at the hip. Each building had alternating areas of red and white paint, giving the illusion of being painted from a template.

On the left side of the building hung a ROUTE 66 highway sign. The abandoned structure sported a white lifeless iron frame overhang which at one time also possessed a red and white striped covering, and had all the appearances of a drive-in. In previous lives, I learned, this hidden piece of nostalgia was known as the Dawg Diner, and more recently Big Al's Hot Dogs.

The best features of the entire building were the support poles on the right side. Painted in candy stripes of red and white they provided a Santa Claus feel even though they might look more at home in front of a barber shop. The building was up for sale. As Route 66 declined over the years, so did the businesses located on it.

Entering Dwight meant taking a trip back in time with streets covered in lush green trees and 1960s era suburbia houses. After passing the town water tower to the right and stopping at a T in the road, a triangular shaped downtown section lay to the left.

Entering Main Street from the backside it had all the wonderful shops and businesses one would come to expect of a small quintessential midwestern town: gift shop, clothing store, restaurant, bank, video store, lawyer's office, real estate office—everything a visitor could ever need. To the right, I observed a small peaceful park with a towering clock.

Parking the car in one of the angular parking spots and meandering over to the Bank of Dwight, a Frank Lloyd Wright designed building, I asked a bank employee for directions to the public library.

"Go down the block to the railroad tracks but don't cross them. Then take a left, go down to the Mansion and it's right there," the bank clerk said, almost bowing her head with religious reverence when she said the word *Mansion*.

I found the Mansion alright. Seeing that it was a yellowish southern plantation style house with an impressive vine-covered English colonial stone house next to it I couldn't help but think to myself, *I need a career change.* Driving around and around, I found the library sitting on the Mansion's backside.

A brown stone 1800s-style building, it looked more like an old-time courthouse than a library. Parking my car, I didn't bother to lock the doors, even though I had my worldly possessions in the back. In small towns like Dwight the need to lock car doors is rare.

Once, in Two Harbors, Minnesota, I had to leave a van-full of merchandise at a gas station for repair. Hustling to lock the doors and reminding the station manager to keep the doors locked, he assured me it wasn't a concern in a town like his: maybe in Minneapolis, but never here. Since then, when in a small friendly town, I seldom have these concerns.

Strange, I thought to myself walking up the sidewalk. I'm here peddling a business book when the focus of the trip is barbeque. Why bother? Perhaps I felt insecurities over not having marketed the book much, and this would make me feel I was taking action. I didn't need the money for the trip, I was well-funded. Insecurities. It must have been the insecurities; I had invested countless hours researching and writing the book, and now, spontaneously, I had a pressing need to get some return on investment. I couldn't just be happy stealing purpose from my current existence.

Regardless of what I thought, the sun shone bright and the sky blazed blue as I reached the front door. I would introduce myself, give a sales pitch, and be on my merry way. Having burned myself in Chicago, I didn't plan on spending much time here, as I was anxious to get going to Springfield. Big-city habits never die.

* * *

Nifty, I thought, upon leaving the library. A mischievous mention of barbeque sparked a familiar transformation: A bright twinkle gleamed in eyes, spoken tones turned more upbeat, body language leaned intensely forward. Furthermore, a barbeque addict, waiting for the right moment, blurted up a BBQ endorsement for the 17th Street Grill near Southern Illinois University, by Carbondale.

Chicago's tragedy seemed to be left in the rear view mirror. My spirits lifted. Walking back down the sidewalk to my car the sun shone brighter and the sky blazed bluer. A mundane effort to peddle a business book in a small town in central Illinois, on The Mother Road, promised the memory of a lifetime. I knew the rest of the day would be great.

Driving two hours from Dwight to Springfield, the weather turned from happy sunshine to grumpy old man, spitting out dark miserable rain. Although numerous iconic Route 66 towns populated the exits, towns like Lincoln and Pontiac, the landscape never seemed to change from vast open prairies sprinkled with an occasional farm.

As the distance to Springfield grew shorter, the prospect of barbeque loomed larger. I left the freeway at the South Grand exit and waited for the light to change at a four-way intersection. A large billboard nagged me to visit the Lincoln Library. I'll see it on the way out, I thought, gotta have ribs.

Driving for eons along South Grand and not seeing Clay's Popeye's BBQ (not to be confused with Popeyes® Louisiana Kitchen, a national fast-food chicken chain, also on South Grand), I figured a mistake had been made. Convenience stores, gas stations, and strip malls soon turned to rows of older houses and forgotten neighborhoods. Although I eventually found Popeye's, the sky remained dark and overcast. It was now noontime.

The outside of Popeye's was brown brick with green trim and large see-through windows. To the left a rough looking neighborhood bar awaited unsuspecting souls.

Walking inside Popeye's, seating booths were to the right with a colorful wall-size mural of a small lake on the prairie during a warm sunny day. The center area held scattered tables. Fluorescent lights lit the dim premises and the walls were constructed of light golden wood slats. A dull pink counter the color of pork sat to the far left with a cash register on the right side. It reminded me of a 1950's era malt shop.

The back contained a Wall of Fame populated with pictures, newspaper articles, awards, plaques, and signs that gave a living history of all things Popeye's. President Bill Clinton and Boxing Champion Muhammad Ali had eaten here. A nephew won a NCAA Weight Lifting Championship, benching 463 pounds, while another was a high school high jump champion. Among the memorabilia hung a smiling picture of Popeye himself, with plaques and awards too numerous to count.

A few customers dotted the tables. Employees mulled about the counter. One, an African-American woman, walked over ready to take my order.

"What would you like?" she asked.

"A half-slab combination platter," I answered, hands trembling from the knowledge that this would be the first barbeque on my tour. "Are you camera shy?" I added. "I know it may sound like a weird question, but I'm on a barbeque tour in search for the perfect barbeque. I am interviewing people along the way for my little YouTube video. Are you open to saying hi to the camera?"

She stood over me in her dark Popeye's apron while I sat in the booth. I'm guessing she was about my height, 5'9", and probably in her thirties. "No," she answered, "I'm totally camera shy. I don't want to be on camera at all, but you could talk to them." She pointed to three people sitting at a far table and then walked over there, engaging them in conversation. When she came back she said, "You can go over there and talk to them now."

Sitting at the table were a middle-aged gentleman and a married couple. Shaking hands, I introduced myself. "Hi. I'm Tim from Minneapolis. I'm on a barbeque tour in search for the perfect barbeque. I'm interviewing people everywhere I go for a fun little YouTube video. The waitress is camera shy, but she suggested I talk to you. Do you mind being on camera?"

"Sure," said the middle-aged gentleman. A White Caucasian in his mid-fifties, he stood of average height and build with his military style short dark hair and wire-rimmed glasses. Adding to that he wore a casual button down checkered shirt and shorts.

Pointing to a photograph of Popeye he stated in a

low deadpan tone, "Me and Ol Popeye shared something in common." Then, tearing into a volume raising Shakespearean crescendo, he demanded I understand the connection between Popeye and him, "Popeye was from Pine Bluff, Arkansas ... and I also lived in Pine Bluff Arkansas," trailing off in whispered silence.

Now most people when they speak don't vary the tone of their voice like a bell-shaped curve. All I could do was stand and absorb the moment, although I managed to ask, "Would you mind introducing yourself to the camera?"

"Sure, my name is Tommy Campbell," instantly striking a pose and turning sideways. Unleashing a Joe Frazier verbal left hook he boomed, "You will *never* eat finer barbeque than you eat right here!" driving his index finger towards the floor. As though apologetic he thrust his hands high in the air with open palms, like after a policeman says, *Put'm up.*

Fantastic, I thought, fiery and unpredictable. I've got the interview of the century. My friends will be jealous. This is more like an interview with Pampero Firpo, the Wild Bull of the Pampas. This is going to go viral.

Fearing to say anything, I clutched the camera with a death grip. "Popeye's recipe is old school," Tommy continued. "It's been passed down through the generations and it's over 100 years old."

Marlon McCoy, my co-worker in Minneapolis, originates from Dallas, Texas. He is a big African-American man, six-feet-three inches tall and weighing in the vicinity of 280 pounds. He hails from a long family blood line that knows the finer points of BBQ. He enters neighborhood contests and wins with his secret rub and secret sauce. He proclaims to anyone who'll listen, "In the neighborhood I'm known as Barbeque Sweets."

I asked Tommy, "What do you have to say to my friend Mr. McCoy, who thinks *he* has the best barbeque?"

Like a lit stick of dynamite Tommy tore into an on-camera diatribe, "McCoy, you don't hold a candle to Popeye's! Come on down and we'll have a cook off and I guarantee you're gonna lose!!" It took me a few seconds to process that Tommy had just challenged McCoy to a cage match—barbeque style.

Tommy jammed his finger into the camera, like a villain, all the while holding a steely stare. "If you want to come on down here and face a cook off," he declared, "call me. I will watch but not judge it because I'm biased because Popeye's is the best there is!"

I stood timid, asking, "Can I bring Sandifer, my other co-worker, too?" Sandifer is six-feet-two inches tall, weighs 250 pounds and has the build of a linebacker, since he used to be one in his Arena Football days.

Tommy retorted, "You just tell all your buddies this barbeque is so good it will make your tongue slip out, stick up, and slap you in the forehead. It's that good." He said this all the while crouched and turned sideways. In a smooth one piece motion he flung his index finger straight out, flicked it up, and finished with a hand *smack* to his forehead. But he just couldn't hide the grin.

Leaving at a fast pace, he returned. Up went his right arm, palm open. "Ain't nuth'n but the truth my friend, nuth'n but the truth," he said, folky like.

Now moving to the cash register, he said, "Ain't nobody touched that cash register but Popeye." Crouching, flinging his left arm out and pointing, he then flung it back. "Ain't nobody touched that machine but Popeye," and he continued flinging his arm out, pointing, and flinging it back.

He had one more thing on his mind. "You just send your buddies on down. We'll show'm two things. Great barbeque, and East Side pride," he tapped his index finger, then tapped it again, "that's what it's all about." With that, Tommy Campbell turned and left.

My plate of ribs sat alone on the table, but they would have to wait. Next came the married couple, Bob and Pauline Haley, the bipolar opposite of Tommy Campbell. They are friends of the Popeye family and had been coming here since the mid 1970s.

Bob noted, "Popeye was a very secretive fellow. He wouldn't even reveal his recipe to the people that worked here. He brought bags filled with different ingredients and mixed them all together himself at the restaurant. The only thing he did reveal is that it contained apples."

Bob and Pauline were prayer partners with Mary and Jeff, the current owners. "We believe in the power of prayer," Pauline said.

"Whenever there is a problem in either family we all pray for each other," Bob added.

Pauline rattled off examples, from insurance problems to housing, where the power of prayer got them through. Their Faith in action shone as bright as the noonday sun. It had to be for me to postpone my plate of ribs.

"You know, I touched Muhammad Ali," I said to Bob, bragging like a smarty pants. In 1980, at the old Met Center in Bloomington, Minnesota, Larry Holmes defended his boxing title against local boxer, Scott LeDoux. Ali was there, and he ran up and down the aisle leading from the dressing room to the ring, promoting his upcoming bout with Holmes. I worked as an usher lining the aisle. As Ali ran by I couldn't resist, and reached out and touched him.

Bob replied, "Well, I talked to him once. I work at the state and he came down to the state office building for his boxing license. My co-worker introduced me to him and we had a nice chat."

Muhammad Ali, *The Greatest of All Time, Float like a Butterfly, Sting like a Bee;* I only touched him, but Bob talked to him. It took a few minutes before the goosebumps simmered down.

Bob's family lived in Louisiana for a while before coming to Illinois. When Bob speaks he does so in a calm

Sunday preacher demeanor. "There's a small barbeque shack in northern Louisiana right on the Mississippi River named Jim's. It's been flooded so many times you can see the watermarks on the walls. They've been there 80 years. Everybody knows them. It's not as good as Popeye's, it's passing barbeque, but I like it."

I wondered what he meant by "passing barbeque." Later, I tried to find a definition for it on the internet, but failed. It didn't matter. Bob held a secret close to his heart that few learned. He isn't the type to reveal it until he's secure in the knowledge that the person he's sharing it with holds the same passion for barbeque that he does. And this was his moment.

Meanwhile, one of the owners, Mary, an African-American in her 60s, a little shorter than me and with a slightly heavier build, walked over wearing a yellow t-shirt, black bandana, and black apron. I peppered her with questions, too, and got more than I bargained for.

"Popeye's has been at this location for 50 years. My grandfather created the recipe in 1889." I learned she'd walked in Civil Rights marches down in Mississippi and Tennessee back in the 1960s. Her courage in those times defies description.

Working, digging, trying like a sleuth to get her to reveal something, anything about their secret sauce she rebuffed me with a firm but polite, "It wouldn't be a secret then, would it?"

Jeff, head cook and co-owner with Mary, his wife, took his own crack at educating my small viewing audience. "We have pork, beef, chicken, and fish too." He wasn't flamboyant like Tommy Campbell, but he more than made up for it by dishing out heavy doses of genteel spirit and hospitality.

When I first approached the table I assumed the three of them were friends. They were not. Bob and Pauline had never met Tommy Campbell before that day. Ever.

49

Mary offered to warm up my ribs. They had been sitting for a long time. My platter included baked beans and coleslaw. The beans were something to write home to mom about; raw, sweet, genuine and authentic. They had a dark brown chunky texture and upon taking the first bite, it didn't take a genius to figure out those were old school too. The coleslaw—to die for—matched the homespun, made from scratch delight like the rest of it; gritty, flavorful, and juicy. The secret sauce, slathered on in heavy doses, made vain attempts to hide its subtleties buried deep in the meaty ribs.

The combination of ribs and sauce carried two stand-out features; the sweetest apple flavor ever, and a smokiness that struck like a CIA spy. Not overpowering, but sneaky and present. I am not a tangy, spicy, vinegar, mustard type of guy. But make no doubt, I enjoy the rich flavor of sweet. That sauce, those ribs—sweet and sneaky.

Former Minnesota Vikings Head Coach, Bud Grant, used to say that the true mark of a Champion was his endurance. If that's the test, then Popeye's and their secret sauce, created not long after Lincoln was assassinated, has endured. They've outlasted the Spanish-American War, two World Wars, Women's Suffrage, the Great Depression, the Industrial Revolution, the Civil Rights Movement, the rise of the internet, Hurricane Katrina, our first black President, the Technology Revolution, the Arab Spring, the Great Recession, and the ever changing nature of our complicated world.

The deep family nature of Popeye's connected with me. When I discovered this family business I had no idea what I'd run into. Now I knew. The gregarious, animated Tommy Campbell. The wholesome honesty of Bob and Pauline. The outsized humbleness of Mary and Jeff. It's not feasible to write a script for my discovery. It just is.

When I look back years from now on that afternoon, I'll have warm fuzzy thoughts. I'll laugh. I'll reflect with honor. I'll be humbled. I'll tell my friends who I met on that afternoon. And I'll brag. There in Springfield sits a neighborhood unique among us. I ate ribs from a 100 old recipe, passed down through generations, with an apple flavor never to be witnessed again. "Top that, get going," I'll tell my friends, "they're waiting for you, and tell'm I said hello."

I forced myself to leave and slapped on the flag helmet—now it was time for the rest of Springfield. I morphed into a tourist, biking to everything possible: the Lincoln-Herndon Law Office, the Old Statehouse, the Lincoln Home, and the Lincoln Visitor center, to name a few. I even scored the name of the media specialist at the Public Library. Honest Abe smiled down on me.

I visualized myself being back in time, asking Lincoln and his partner, Herndon, a tough law question in their long skinny downtown office or debating him in the chamber at the Statehouse with far more ferocity than Douglas ever did.

I imagined Abe, his wife Mary, and their kids taking a Sunday stroll along the dirt road in front of their home. I would say, "Hi Mr. President. How are you doing?"

"Fine son, have a great day," he would say in his slow, folksy speak, and continue on.

Today, the Lincoln Visitor Center is one of the hidden treasures of American travel. It educates and entertains with gentle spirit, dispensing history with the ease and intrigue of the Rail Splitter himself.

Tried by War: Lincoln as Commander in Chief by James M. McPherson, hid innocently on their bookstore's plain shelves. Since I had finished reading *Churchill*, I needed something else to pass the time. This filled the bill.

"Whooooey, yeeehhaaah, yipppeeee!" Another victory dance in the car seat, my arms raised in celebration, whooping, hollering, and cheering—I was driving on Route 66, again. Eventually reaching highway

55 and accelerating to speed I kicked myself for not allowing time to visit the Lincoln Library, "Oh well. I can't do everything."

Gliding down the highway, the landscape didn't change from field upon field of open grassy plains with the occasional clump of trees. On the other side of the Illinois' plains stood the city of St. Louis with its horrible reputation for crime and violence, making me want to camp 25 to 30 miles this side of its outer limits. In fact, internet research showed that St. Louis was number one in violent crimes in the whole country—worse than Detroit.

Another co-worker of mine, a St. Louis native, didn't know much about barbeque places there, but pushed hard for Erio's Pizza. In addition, the Cardinals had a baseball game at Busch Stadium this coming weekend.

The mounting pressure of always being in a rush took its toll as questions ping ponged inside my head. Do I see the Cardinals game tonight or tomorrow? Will I be successful in marketing my business book to the public library? Where is the public library? What tourist things should I do? When do I visit the Arch? Do I even visit the Arch? When do I eat barbeque? Where do I eat barbeque? When do I bike? Where do I bike? Do I stop at Carbondale and try the barbeque there? Where is Carbondale? Do I eat barbeque tonight and pizza tomorrow? Or pizza tonight and barbeque tomorrow?

Adding to my frustration was the inevitable curse of more road construction. The sign ahead pointed out an alternate route. "How bad could it be?" I mused. Bad. 50 miles of chest-wailing, tear-inducing road construction. *50 miles.*

I wasn't the only poor sap to skip the detour. The tangle of motorists stranded in this infinite two lane parking lot was proof. As I surrendered to the situation, calm took over.

And then a weird mathematical oddity occurred.

Springfield had a freakish high density of campgrounds. But the closer I got to St. Louis, the more the density decreased with each approaching exit. To say it another way: the further from the small town and the closer to the big city I came, the density of campgrounds inverted. Odd.

I did note two brain-teasing events along this stretch of road construction. First, traffic came to a complete stop, moving at 0 miles per hour with a posted maximum speed limit of 65. Second, each vehicle went around something. This puzzled me; it couldn't be a slow-moving motorist for we were all slow moving motorists.

Approaching the something, I shook my head in dismay. On this bright sunny day, with blue skies and sizzling hot temperatures, a large twisted pile of metal spanked the cursed cement.

In fact, it was a five-car pileup: "One, two, three, four, five." I saw humanity exit vehicle number five, the large black SUV, at an accelerated clip, barely imagining so many could be packed into so small a space. That vehicle's front end sported a newfound accordion structure, with its hood bent straight up towards the sky. No other vehicles experienced similar damage, suffering mere love taps instead.

One African-American, a twentysomthing fellow, plopped himself in the middle of the freeway. Sitting down, legs outstretched, he rested his elbows on the cement with no visible inclination to move. I thought his buttocks would burn from the sizzling hot cement. He eventually stood up and rubbed his back with vigor. Various clusters of motorists passed pieces of paper between themselves at a frantic pace, while showing serious faces.

I eventually got around them and accelerated to a state of slow motion. A few miles down the road I found a sign that read CAMPING EXIT 23. Exiting and following the frontage road to the RV Park, I hopped out and looked up. There it was, taped to the door—a standard sheet of paper.

Deciphering the scribble, I read the traumatizing words, NO TENTS ALLOWED. Campers were now reduced to second-class citizen status because we want to follow a centuries-old tradition of sleeping in tents. With head hanging low and sagging shoulders I did a slow shuffle to the car. I steered down the road as unintelligible babble, disguised as words, dribbled out of my mouth.

On trips I rely on internet customer reviews to help make decisions. What else is there to go on? Doing basic research at a McDonald's off exit 11 in Collinsville, a St. Louis suburb, two camping options presented themselves: A KOA campground close to the original Route 66, and Cahokia RV Park.

I was excited about option number one until I read their dismal reviews, filled with too many comments such as *worst place I have ever stayed at* or *I will never stay there again*. I saw a lot of one word adjectives like *dirty*, *unkempt*, and *horrible*. That cemented it. Other experiences at KOA campgrounds were an influence. They don't have any late night registration options, and they have those darn uninviting gates that boldly state, *Don't stay here,* so I don't.

On the opposite end of the spectrum, the Cahokia RV Park had a friendly voice on their recording who went out of her way to welcome travelers, saying that late-night registration was no problem and they had lots of room—welcome to all.

I often rail against the intrusions of technology and how it has turned our society into a self-centered, instant gratification crowd of me-first snobs. On trips I deny technology as I seek to become one with nature, yet here at McDonald's the other side of technology reared its head. Oh, the convenience, the simplicity, the usefulness of the information that its WiFi transmitted.

Needing directions to the RV park, a McDonald's employee, a technology hero, whipped out his Smartphone and showed me a MapQuest® map. He saved the day by dispensing tactical directions with the ever-nimble swipe of his finger.

Further internet research for the best barbeque in St. Louis turned up three names: Pappy's, Roper's, and Bogart's. Bogart's didn't have many reviews, while the other two had numerous reviews. After looking at their respective websites, I found Roper's left something to be desired and didn't work right, while Pappy's was slick and attractive to the eye. Pappy's it was then.

Cahokia RV Park was all that it was advertised to be and then some. Registering via their night-registration box went off without a hitch. After setting up the tent, I made a mental note in regard to the curious barbeque restaurant right in the campground.

Next, mental gyrations flourished on whether to have ribs or pizza that night. Choosing pizza and calling Erio's for directions, a voice on the other end struggled to give them. After much wrangling, another employee took the phone, assuring me with decided confidence that it wouldn't be possible for me to make it there (near Lambert International airport) before they closed. The clock read 8:45 pm. They closed at 10:30 pm. Geez, I thought, St. Louis must be really spread out, like a vast urban desert, maybe like Houston or Dallas.

"What are your hours tomorrow, Saturday?"

"4 pm to 11 pm."

Planning to leave St. Louis well before 4 pm, my Erio's dream dwindled by the second, so Plan B went into effect. Yet, my stoic desire to eat at Erio's put up a fight. My co-worker did a good job burning Erio's into my subconscious.

Scheming and wracking my brain for a solution, surely a bite of pizza would be within grasp. No solution appeared possible and a pity party ensued. Despite the fact the theme of my trip was barbeque, I was caught up in a tangent. And so I concluded: eat pizza in downtown! The beauty lay in that downtown existed five minutes away, right on the other side of the mighty Mississippi River.

Driving over the bridge, the cheerful lights of Busch Stadium, home of the St. Louis Cardinals, greeted all. Together the stadium lights formed a powerful beam shooting into the night sky. Its brown brick and black ironwork created an imposing figure peering in all directions. Endorphines released in mass over the idea of seeing a baseball game.

Not far in the distance the St. Louis Arch, a tribute to our early explorers, painted the evening skyline, evoking a range of emotions: comfort, joy, and inspiration. The Gateway to the West.

It didn't take long to find a place to satisfy my hunger pangs. I spotted Maurizio's Pizza & Pasta Bowl, only a few blocks from the stadium and across the street from Hooters. Of course, Hooters had nothing to do with my decision to eat at Maurizio's (*wink, wink*); I was motivated by the purest of intentions.

Arriving at 10 pm they had more the appearance of a bar than a pizzeria, the walls painted a dark pool table green. But the aroma captured my soul the second I stepped in.

A real bar was to the right, with a large flat panel TV mounted high on the wall behind it. A scattering of tables littered the center area while a smattering of booths jostled the left and front walls.

I placed an order with the man in the back. Italian sausage with green peppers, onions, and pineapple, thin crust—all for a more than reasonable ten dollars. When I added pineapple to my order I could hear the folks nearby whisper *yuk* behind my back.

The man in the back wore a grey Maurizio's t-shirt, jeans, and a Cardinals hat. He had an ease about him that stirred relaxation. I tend to ask a lot of questions, and tonight was no exception. I asked, "How big is a small? Is a medium super-big or is it only a little larger than small? Do you have pineapple? Where is Pappy's? Do you have deep dish? Do you have WiFi here? Is there a Cardinals game tomorrow? If so, what time?"

With each question he smiled patiently and did his best to answer. He made ordering pizza fun. He explained the options and assured me I could have anything I wanted on my pizza. No, they didn't have WiFi, but it was possible to tap into the hotel across the street. He had seen other patrons do it, but it was spotty, and he offered me several WiFi codes to try.

He confirmed the Cardinals game the next night was at 6:15 pm. My original plan was to leave St. Louis around noon on Saturday, arriving in Kansas City around 5 pm to spend the night gorging on barbeque before traveling back to Minneapolis on Sunday. Dilemma: attending the game would lead to a marathon driving day on Sunday which would inevitably cause innumerable headaches. Something unforeseen always happens.

The pizza arrived and it tasted as good as it looked. The sausage had the right amount of spiciness, a nice kick to it, but not enough to result in a desperate gasp for water. Whitish cheese flowed over the entire pizza like a soft winter snow covering an open field. The texture and taste set off an explosion of satisfaction similar to how one might feel upon reaching the top of Mount Everest. They used the right amount of green peppers, onions, and pineapple; proportion is everything. And the collage of colors made it extra inviting, like the lure of a pretty woman.

The crust had the correct thickness—firm, not flimsy. Taking a bite, it also had the proper amount of crunchy. A great pizza is defined by its crust. Quality ingredients in pizza dough excite the happy nerves.

Like great ribs, the combination of ingredients made eating here a spiritual experience. Mix in the Diet Coke and I asked myself, *Why do I have to leave? If Erio's is to die for then what's this?* This pizza was by far the best pizza I'd eaten in a long, long, time. Oblivious to worry and freedom from the external world, a wonderful state of being had been achieved, all because of pizza.

Using those superior multitasking skills I have been blessed with, I took a few bites of pizza, followed by the removal of my laptop from the backpack, a firing up of the word processor, and a few words typed for the draft of this book.

After a few more bites, I pulled out the new book I'd purchased in Springfield, *Tried by War: Lincoln as Commander in Chief,* and started reading. The pages flew by at an uncontrollable rate. After a while I stopped reading, took a few more bites of pizza, typed a few more words on the laptop for my draft, and decided screw it— Lincoln was just too fascinating.

Getting back to Cahokia was easy; drive to the Arch, hang a right, get on I-70 East, go over the bridge, exit at highway 3, curve right, drive straight three miles, and there's the campground with its promise of soulful sleep.

But emerging from the curve off exit 3, I caught a glimpse of a silhouette of buildings to the right with bright captivating neon signs. Curiosity reached out and grabbed me. Investigating, the naked realization hit that I was in the seductive naughty zone of East St. Louis. Temptation circled, luring at every opportunity; morality weakened by the second with lust following close behind.

And then something else seized my attention. In the distance, among the neon signs and shadowy silhouettes, cavernous barbeque smokers dotted the parking lots, manned by generously rotund gentlemen working their craft with profound authority. Soft puffs of smoke rose in the crisp cool nighttime air carrying the scintillating scent of sweet barbeque to the senses, destroying all power to resist.

CHAPTER 5

mr y got his groove

Crawling out of the tent at sunrise on this Saturday morning, I found menacing skies lurking above. Murmuring, "*Oh oh, this doesn't look good,*" I felt the first dribbles of rain hit while jumping in the car to drive the 200 feet to the main building. How strange, rushing to take a shower in order to avoid getting wet. As I took the first step onto the porch a downpour erupted. Moments later bursts of lightning strafed the sky. Stone-crushing thunder followed. Tornado sirens blared.

Opening a door marked RESTROOM and rushing in, I saw a balding man standing in front of a mirror, a towel wrapped around his waist. A light wind could have sent him twirling with ease. Shaving cream covered his face, failing to hide the wrinkles.

"Where do we go when tornado sirens are blaring?" I asked, ready to bolt, my words coming in jumbled spurts.

"Ah, those are nuth'n, I've lived here 11 years ... those don't mean much, I don't bother with'm." He continued shaving without a care in the world.

"In Minnesota, where I come from, tornado sirens mean something. They mean take cover, now."

"Ah, those are nuth'n."

The sirens stopped after 15 minutes. My purpose this morning was to take a shower and it was time to take care of the dirty business of getting clean. Catching a glimmer of a bar of soap where the old man had been, the devious part of me took it figuring he would never notice, placing it in my shower stall before heading back to the car to get a few things.

Outside on the porch I ran into Glen. He's a couple inches taller than me and he comes from Elvis' hometown of Tupelo, Mississippi. He spoke with a recognizably southern drawl. Donning a black t-shirt, wire-rimmed glasses, and a plain black baseball hat, he sported a medium whitish beard. He too was hiding from the weather. We talked about the sort of thing strangers do when surviving early morning thunderstorms— barbeque, of course.

A close friend of Glen's dreams of going on a BBQ Tour in North Carolina. Having traveled to North Carolina before I'm not fond of the vinegar and mustard-based sauces they use. Glen isn't fond of them either. I like sweet, and Glen likes sweet too.

Nancy, Glen's wife, came and joined the conversation. With short brunette hair, she was a little taller than me, but a little shorter than Glen. She emitted southern down-home warmth and friendliness. She reminded me of the mom of a high school friend. "In Mississippi everyone ignores the sirens too," she said, "except the last time everyone ignored them, the big storm hit and they got wiped out. Now I just jump." Upon saying that, she went inside.

"You should write an article about your tour," Glen said in that slow southern drawl.

Right then an air-to-ground lightning strike flashed a short distance away. *"WOOOOO!"* I yelled, jumping a foot or two. The dim light above flickered like in a Hitchcock movie. The creepiness set me back on my heels. More stone-crushing thunder arrived seconds later.

"I've been really close to a lightning strike before. You can just feel it, the power of it, the shockwave. It just hurts," Glen said, calm as a cucumber.

At that exact moment a mighty lightning bolt

exploded in the sky in the near distance. Its brilliant flash painted the morning air, triggering a momentary blindness. A split-second later, all of earth shook from the *KABOOM!!* The deafening blast lingered, refusing to leave.

"I'm outta here!" I said, squealing like a scared pig. "I'm not gonna get nailed by lightning." I ran to the nearest door, about a foot away. Glen followed close behind. Nancy, already there, jumped up and down letting out her own squeals.

Once the storm subsided and we gathered our wits, Nancy threw in her two cents worth about her favorite barbeque spots, "There's the 17th Street Grill or something like that in Murphysboro, and there's this place in Memphis ...."

The 17th Street Grill sounded decidedly familiar. That was the place the person in Dwight, Illinois, had talked so highly about. But for the best barbeque ribs anywhere Nancy's money was on Rendezvous in Memphis.

It is impossible to have a conversation about barbeque and not mention Memphis, Tennessee. Memphis-style ribs are the pillar of barbeque. They're iconic, the very foundation of an entire culture.

After a quick goodbye to Glen and Kathy I headed back inside to take a shower. But something seemed wrong. My bar of soap had vanished. He had seemed so innocent and carefree standing in front of the mirror shaving. Somewhere in all the chaos he had slipped in, stealth-like, and re-acquired it. That Old Dog, he got me.

Back at the tent, the pitter patter of raindrops fell uninterrupted. Memories of close encounters with monstrous storms played in my head, especially during the previous summer in Louisville, Kentucky. They were the worst.

Camping 20 miles north of Louisville, at Charlestown State Park in Indiana, it was the weekend of the city's annual *Balloon Glow and Race*, and the balloons were anchored on the other side of a clump of trees next to my campsite. They sat suspended in the air like rainbow colored puffs, dotting the sky. On that gorgeous clear evening the constant *phhhssssttt* infiltrated the air as each balloonist pulled a lever unleashing a blast of flame. The crowds bustled from balloon to balloon gawking in awe, savoring the sweet smells of beer and hotdogs.

As I headed to sleep, the Master of Ceremonies could be heard announcing over the bullhorn, "What a beautiful evening it's going to be. The forecast for tomorrow is absolutely beautiful!" His glee locked away all rational thinking, until raindrops attacked at 3 am. Forced to get up, I staggered in the dark to the car, got the rain cover, and attached it to the tent. I crawled back inside the tent and attempted to fall asleep.

Then it started. Lightning strikes. Everywhere. I lived in denial and believed they were strobe lights from the balloons. I became a believer when monstrous thunder blasts shook the ground. Torrential rains crashed from the skies. Howling winds swirled and roared. Trees swayed at angles free from the laws of geometry, ready to snap and fall, delivering their promise of pain and destruction. In the midst of the chaos I observed *Eureka!* (printed on the tent flap cover) twisting and flapping in ways that fail even a remote description; my own version of *Amityville Horror*. Mother Nature went for the knockout blow, but that amazing little tent refused to go down.

In the morning truth prevailed. Four massive storms had converged on Indiana, Ohio, and Kentucky, spawning record-setting tornados that left epic destruction in their paths. Henryville, only 10 miles away, was destroyed in the blink of an eye. Me? I got spared.

Memories of those storms persisted while I fell back asleep in Cahokia. Re-awakening later in the morning, I was grateful a Higher Power looked down on me from above.

My main goal today would be to pig out on barbeque. Visiting the restaurant in the campground seemed too easy, but Pappy's fit the bill. The Old Dog shuffled by slow in the parking lot. "See, I told you it was nuth'n to worry about." His grin stretched from ear-to-ear.

Thoughts about the mundane grind of everyday life back home in Minneapolis drifted into the distant past. The current moment had zip, zest, appeal, moxie, and every other adjective that uplifts the emotions.

Heading to downtown, parking, and then pedaling over to Busch Stadium to purchase a ticket to the Cardinals game became priority number one. Having been burned by a scalper during the World Series in San Francisco a few years ago, I took no chances. The unapologetic beauty and immensity of Busch Stadium, a modern day baseball coliseum, leaves the everyday man gawking in awe.

Legions lingered throughout the stadium plaza early in the afternoon; strange, since the game didn't start until 6:15 pm. In the 1970s, Baseball Game of the Week played on TV every Saturday afternoon. The Cardinals were frequently featured. They always opened the broadcast with Joe Garagiola booming, "BASEBALL! AMERICAN STYLE!" As a little tyke I used to imitate him, yelling into a make believe mike at the top of my lungs.

Statues of former St. Louis Cardinals greats dotted the plaza real estate: Lou Brock, Bob Gibson, Stan Musial, and Dizzy Dean, to name a few. Lou Brock was the greatest base stealer of all time; once he got on base you took it for granted that he was going to take off. He ran with the grace of a deer—effortless and smooth. Opposing pitchers had no chance of keeping him on the bag and catchers couldn't ever make their throws in time.

Bob Gibson had the most feared fastball of his time and outright dominated opponents whenever he took the mound. He stared down batters with a look that could burn holes through steel. In my youth I always found myself pretending to be him, hurling the tennis ball like a rocket against the garage door. Imaginary batters always went down swinging with a drafty swoosh of the bat. Musial and Dean were an earlier generation, but they both possessed an enduring talent that transcends time.

The gentleman in front of me in line attempted to work a hustle. "No," I said firmly and forcefully, "I'm going to buy my ticket from the ticket window. Thanks anyways."

At the ticket booth the clerk giggled, "You're a long ways from home. You sure have come far to see a baseball game." More giggles.

"I sure am. I'm on a barbeque tour in search of the perfect barbeque. But I can't come this far and not see a Cardinals game. Lucky me. I'm trying to find Pappy's Barbeque. The pizza guy last night told me it was downtown, not too far from here. Do you know where it is?"

"Oh no, they are a long ways away. You should go to Bogart's instead. They are a satellite restaurant of Pappy's and their ribs are the same."

"Are they close?"

"Yep, just take this street right in front of the stadium over to Broadway, take another right, go under the bridge and keep going until you get to Lafayette. Then take a left, and there they are."

"Great, I'm going there then. Go Cardinals." I said, adding a snicker doodle giggle of my own.

I rode to the Arch first. It sits in a vast green park on the eastern edge of downtown, right on the western bank of the Mississippi river. The park is officially named the Jefferson National Expansion Memorial. It was built to honor America's early explorers on their way to fame and fortune—the Gateway to the West.

Designed as a weighted inverted catenary curve, by definition, it forms the curve of a hanging chain. It took 16 years to build at a cost of $13 million. Due to politics, like most landmarks, the process to get to the point of making it took forever, including a long miserable process that involved relocating railroad tracks. Its outside is a stainless steel skin covering two carbon steel walls reinforced in its center with concrete up to 300 feet from its base. Both the width and the height of the Arch stand at 630 feet. A nice feature is that it is earthquake resistant.

Riding near it, under it, and around it to recruit other tourists to work my camera proved to be no challenge. My flag helmet started the necessary conversations, including ardent dialogue with Kerry and Crystal, hailing from Texas City, Texas, a suburb of Houston. Kerry wore a black t-shirt with the words "TEXAS CITY" printed in large letters. He looked construction-worker strong with his thick neck, husky shoulders, and whisker-stubbled chin. Crystal, a little shorter, looked suburbanite with medium length dark brown hair and a tight-fitting gray top. Like Kerry, she donned sunglasses.

They were on a mission to see a baseball game in Chicago. I gave them veteran advice. "Don't see the White Sox, see the Cubs instead. They play at Wrigley Field on the north end of Chicago and the area is a lot more fun. There's lots of shops, bars and restaurants and you don't have to worry about getting stabbed either."

They agreed to be interviewed for my video log. Kerry's barbeque establishment of choice is Rudy's Barbeque in Spring, Texas. Standing as a couple facing the camera, he spoke void of emotion like Jack Friday in *Dragnet*. Inching the camera Crystal's direction, she simply pointed her thumb at Kerry and said, "I'm with him."

On the simple mention of Memphis-style ribs, Kerry transformed from Jack Friday into Stone Cold Steve Austin, pacing back and forth like a pissed off lion: arms flailing, jaw clenched, and hurling proclamations to no one in particular. "Memphis-style ribs with their dry rub and minuscule amount of sauce suck. With Texas ribs you can actually taste the meat and the ribs are drenched in sauce. Everyone else uses pork, which aren't real ribs. In Texas we use real ribs made of *real* beef." Paralyzed, I didn't say a peep. After he calmed down, we took pictures of each other. I admired his technique of using his baseball hat to block the glare.

I said my goodbyes and rode off to explore further. *She's got the perfect vantage point for painting the Arch*, I thought, upon seeing Joan Parker, from Kansas City. She looked to be in her forties or maybe even early fifties. Her short blond hair tried to blow in the wind, except the light greenish teal baseball hat on her head wouldn't permit it. Conversation flowed as smooth as the water next to us.

"Gates? Oh no. Don't go to Gates. That's a run-of-the mill chain," she said.

"Where should I go then?" I felt limp and dejected. My co-worker at school represented Gates in Kansas City as the best barbeque anywhere. Now this woman was saying that they're no good.

Leaning her elbows on the break wall, she added, "Well I think Arthur Bryant's is your first choice, the best —and it's second generation. The daughter's running it now and it's absolutely terrific. You have to stand in line to get through. You've got to get the ribs, maybe try a little bit of everything. Oklahoma Joe's (now Joe's Kansas City) is a gas station with a line that's always out the door. You can order ahead of time, but then you would miss the room and the gas station itself. We have friends from New York who always beg us to ship ribs to them from Arthur Bryant's."

The fact she lived in Kansas City boosted her credibility far above my co-workers. Her confidence and insider knowledge made decision-making easy. Her friend's begging for Arthur Bryant's became the straw that broke the camel's back. No going to Gates. The time had come for my next destination: Bogart's. I pedaled over to Broadway and headed left.

Directions always seem so easy when they're given, but sadly disappointing when it comes time to carry them out. Biking down Broadway, I stopped for directions. The distance sure seemed a lot further than just "Go under the bridge and take another left."

The clerk at the convenience store didn't know much. "Oh, just go straight for a while and you'll see it." I churned the pedals round and round, like a race car making laps until coming across Soulard's Farmers Market, a bustling marketplace on South Broadway. By this point South Broadway merged into and became South 7th Street.

The hustle and bustle of the Farmer's Market piqued my attention, drawing me to it. Clusters of humans moved like bees to honey. I thrived on the action there. The colors and sweet aromas brought it to life. The beehive of activity brought me to life.

Keep going until you get to Lafayette. Then take a left, and there they are.

Riding for a long time that seemed like forever, I longed for the sweet taste of ribs. Making the left as instructed and pedaling down a street, then back up, then down another street, then back up, I couldn't find Bogart's

My shoulders slumped, my head sagged, and I seethed on the inside. "C'mon, where's Bogart's?" I said, punchy, looking for something to kick without hurting my toe. I squeezed the handlebars until my knuckles turned white. "Crap, they are going to close on me. I came all this way and I'm going to miss them." I despised the clerk at the stadium. *Damn her*.

Options were limited. Popping into Jimmy John's, the clerk there, another technology hero, had an air of confidence about him. His smile and pleasant tone gave him away. Whisking out a Smartphone, he popped up a map of the area and pointed to the red star on the screen. "There it is, Bogart's, only a few blocks back up the street. You're real close," he said.

"The clerk lady told me to take a left, but really I should have taken a right."

"Yup. Just go back up the street, cross over South 7th, and Bogart's is close by."

Following his directions, I biked over into Soulard Park itself. The crowds, the life, the action, ignited my DNA. In the park sat an old restored warehouse. Capitalism thrived at its finest; vendors overflowed, hawking their wares like the shameless promoters they were. Multitudes of shops sold anything that one could ever need. The crowds moved to and fro within the park, shopping, eating, and doing what people do when enjoying a bright sunny afternoon. On the other side of the street to the left, sat an interesting brown brick building, housing what looked to be an abandoned library that might have come from an earlier century.

Bogart's was located across the street from the park, on the far west end, at the intersection of Lafayette and South 9th Street. On all sides of it were gift shops, restaurants, and drinking establishments. Colorfully dressed people buzzed along the sidewalks. Entering shops empty handed, they came out all smiles, clutching shopping bags filled to the brim. Cars and trucks crowded the sleepy streets while the lights at the intersection directed traffic with effortless ease.

From the front, Bogart's looked like a saloon from the 1800s, reminiscent of the French Quarter of New Orleans. The air bounced with old time Cajun honky-tonk music. On the left side of the building were large wooden tables that formed a picnic area. Spacious tan awnings protected the tables from the glaring sun. A long line snaked out the door and zigzagged around the corner. An agreeable air of electricity pulsated through the establishment. Being a schmoozer, opportunities abounded.

Approaching the nearest employee, I announced, "Excuse me, I'm on a trip, on a barbeque tour. Would you be willing to let me interview you with my camera?"

"I'm sorry, I can't right now, I'm really swamped. I will later though."

I snaked along in line and explored the abundance of memorabilia. Everything from the stuffed animals to the pictures suggested Old West saloon. In fact, it seemed like any moment a cowboy could appear with six shooters at his side, winking and asking, *How ya doin' partner?*

At the ordering counter the chatty clerk processed my order with smooth efficiency. He smiled a lot, engaging in small talk as he reviewed each item step-by-step, double checking to make sure he got it right. Handing me a cup, he said, "The soda machine is right over there. Sit wherever you want. Your server will bring your order to you."

I picked one of the wooden picnic tables outside covered by an awning. It provided cool relief from the baking sun. A woman approached and asked, "Would you mind moving over a table? We have a large group."

I answered, "No problem," adding a heavy dose of Minnesota Nice. After moving one table to the left, into the sun, I cooked like a bratwurst with sweat streaking my face. Why did I agree to this, I thought. Why?

She got a kick out of my flag helmet. That and the difficulty I experienced trying to eat the ribs with the darn thing on. I shot her a thin sarcastic grin, but it didn't make any difference. She didn't even try to understand the kluge of wires coming from my laptop.

"I'm from Minneapolis," I said, trying to start a conversation.

"You sure are a long way from home," she said, giggling—like the clerk at the stadium.

"I'm on a BBQ Tour in search for the perfect barbeque."

She bolted up from the table. "You have to meet the people I'm with. I'll be right back." She disappeared into the blaring sun. I didn't fully grasp the moment, but figured she was just being kind to a stranger.

In the meantime the server delivered a plate of generous ribs. They had an orange tint I hadn't seen before. The sides were nothing to sneeze at either. The small dish of dark brown baked beans looked luxurious, befitting a king. Golden fruity applesauce glistened in the sun.

The woman returned with her group. "This is Tim from Minneapolis. He's on a barbeque tour."

What I heard next, I didn't see coming. Mike, her husband, spoke. "The name of our barbeque team is the Pit Stop BBQ. It consists of John, Jeff, and myself. We've been in about half a dozen barbeque competitions over the last couple of years. Last weekend, we got seventh place as a team in the Harris Barbeque Competition." *Is this for real?* I felt the love. That and I was the big man on campus, at least for a few fleeting moments.

The best one word description I can think of for the Pit Stop BBQ team is suburbanites. White Caucasian, squeaky clean, corporate looking, like they just got off the golf course. I attempted to explain to them the nature of my five-day BBQ Tour. All they could do was chuckle in amusement.

On this very day, at this very restaurant, at this very picnic table was Jeff's moment. Like the person in Dwight, Bob in Springfield, and Nancy from Tupelo, he waited, bidding his time, for the right moment to share his favorite barbeque establishments: the 17th Street Grill in Murphysboro; a place in Dexter, Missouri; Salt Lick and County Line, both in Austin, Texas.

Out of sheer curiosity I asked, "What's the name of the place in Dexter?"

"Look it up on the internet," came back his reply.

The 17th Street Grill sounded decidedly familiar. He was the third barbeque addict on my trip to mention it. Given that random people in random locations everywhere have mentioned it, there had to be something to this place.

Salt Lick's reputation precedes them far and wide. It's one of those places every diehard barbeque purist knows about and agrees on. Sort of like how every mathematician knows about the Pythagorean Theorem. They inherently accept it as fact.

"What's the difference between St. Louis style ribs and Memphis Style ribs and for that matter baby back ribs?" I asked.

Mike, much in the manner of a distinguished professor of barbeque history, rolled out a lesson in BBQ 101. "St. Louis style ribs are a bigger cut of rib. The term can refer to both the cut and the rub, which leaves a shiny glaze, thus giving rise to the term wet rub. Memphis-style ribs have a dry rub that gives it a flat look."

Jeff took over with veteran knowledge. "The steer has different rib sizes from large to small, much like human ribs. The St. Louis-style ribs are the bigger ribs, while the baby backs are the smaller, more tender ribs that have more meat."

Mike assigned homework, "There's another joint in Kansas City, called the Jack Stack BBQ, and if you go there you gotta get the burnt ends."

Never again could anyone talk smack to Mr. Y. I passed BBQ 101 with flying colors, learning more about barbeque in those few moments than some learn in a lifetime. I graded myself an A+. Mr. Y. got his groove, baby.

Digging in, those ribs looked mighty good and there looked to be a lot of them for only a half-slab. Plus, the baked beans were awesome. They were sweet, yet barbeque-tasting, similar to the ribs. This couldn't be a mere coincidence.

The applesauce, to die for. It had a golden glittery glow with a tinge of brown powdery spicy something-or-other in it. Sweet to the taste, it woke up the senses.

I had never seen ribs with this kind of orange glow before. From the first bite they owned a slight sweet, fruity, almost tangy flavor with a minute amount of spiciness thrown it.

I struggled to make a decision on which sauce to try; there were simply too many to choose from. It's like going to a chocolate store and having to pick just one. Why make a decision when I don't have to. Instead, I plopped a different sauce into each corner of the plate. In the end Pineapple Express stole the show.

I applied the lessons I learned in BBQ 101. These ribs were St. Louis Style Ribs with wet rub. By themselves they weren't overpowering. True to what I learned, the meat was a little tougher than baby back ribs. The bones weren't as meaty either.

The rub gave them a subtle flavor. Not smokey, but a slight tangy fruity taste. The full weight of the experience relied on the combined force of ribs and sauce. The integrated teamwork of both made it happen. No doubt about it—the sauces were the defining key.

I looked like a dork wearing my flag helmet. I didn't care. Concerns ceased to exist. I boogied to the beat of the music and chowed down with purpose. I wasn't mad at the clerk at the stadium anymore. I loved everyone again.

When I first walked inside to place my order, a big hulk of a man loomed large near the front door. Twice my size, with big arms and big thighs, dressed in a black shirt, baseball hat, and apron, he didn't smile or move, never saying a word to anyone. He just stood there. This is strange, I thought. Since when did they hire bouncers at a barbeque place?

I toyed with the idea of interviewing him. Forget it. I'm not gonna get torn in two—but giving up wasn't an option either. I approached the earlier employee, my server, for another go at it. This time he said, "Sure, now's a good time." Mike Macchi, was of Italian nationality. Unassuming, of average build, he along with three other partners had started Bogart's. "We all just wanted to do something on our own and try a couple of different items other than the usual barbeque. We're offering pastrami and prime rib. We're doing our barbeque ribs a little bit differently, too."

"Cool."

"But we're still heavily involved with Pappy's."

"How long have you been here?"

He unleashed a broad smile, "Four months now."

"Four months now?" The words blurted out. Persisting, "How's business?"

He smiled, and in a grateful tone, not rushing the words, said, "We've been very fortunate. Business is very good."

I probed him for the secret to their success. I expected for him to blabber about their grand list of ingredients and brag about the ingenious way they mix them together.

"Good food, good barbeque, good prices," he said. The simplicity of his statement left me speechless, which is hard to do.

After a pause I said, "I'm going to Kansas City next. I keep hearing about the Big three: Oklahoma Joe's, Jack Stack, and Arthur Bryant's."

"When I go to Kansas City I go to Jack Stacks," he said, more as a point of information.

Wow, I thought, even the owner of an immensely popular barbeque establishment in St. Louis frequents one of the Big Three in Kansas City. I thanked him for the interview and went to unlock my bike.

My trip now had genuine purpose and true meaning. I had run into good fortune that day: Bogart's, the Pit Stop BBQ team ... everyone. *Thank you, St. Louis.*

CHAPTER 6

now what?

With my belly's barbeque cravings satisfied for the day the time had come for the other adventurous stuff that make a trip fun: like kill time until the Cardinals game. On the way back to downtown, strangers shot me strange puzzling glares. It didn't matter if my pedals were spinning at a high rate of speed or my entire bike was at a complete halt, those looks kept coming. The kind that says *there is something wrong with you.*

Whenever this happens, it takes a while before my subconscious mind accepts that the person is looking at me, igniting an emotional struggle. *Do I have crap on my face? Do I have a deformity I don't know about? What?* Suddenly, a light bulb goes off. How silly! The flag helmet, made by Nutcase®. Every city, every park, every sidewalk, every road, every street corner ignites the same emotional struggle, feeding a flame of self-doubt. Never learning from the experience makes biking fun; I love the attention.

Arguably, the best form of transportation for exploring an urban setting is the bicycle. It's cheap, convenient, and easy to park, not to mention the exercise benefits. It's perhaps man's greatest invention.

I burned with desire to experience every nook and cranny of downtown St. Louis. I freed myself from the serious business of life, after having shoveled down great barbeque. Unhinging the urban explorer within, I flew up and down tar pavements with abandon, spinning those pedals round and round. Traffic on this Saturday afternoon was at a minimum; there'd be no curb scraping today. The business district looked like any other business district with streets wrapped by tall shadowy buildings.

Every now and then a sign declared St. Louis to be bike friendly and pointed to a bike route. The sign set the bar high and made it seem a special bike path existed just for me. But with disturbing frequency this wasn't the case. More often than not the bike route was the street directly in front. If there was a real bike path it was short, real short—embarrassing. I've been spoiled by long spacious modern bike paths that wind through lush trees and green fields along gleaming lake shores.

Hope sprang eternal that writing of my daily journal would begin. Up to then, I'd written nothing. The only thing to show for good intentions was optimism. Somewhere along this two-wheeled path there had to be a place of inspiration to draw out the creative genius.

There was a Starbucks coffee shop located on the north end of downtown, across the street from the American Center. Their air-conditioning saved the day because the sweat soaking my head, arms, feet, and butt showed no sign of letting up.

It seemed to take forever to order a Chocolate Banana smoothie. I took it with me on a new search, the kind that couldn't wait any longer. An urgency to go to the bathroom demanded I leave now.

Finding it was no easy task. The Starbucks connected to a fancy five-star hotel with numerous hallways and cavernous rooms, not to mention the challenge of deciphering a cornucopia of floors. The Sheriffs Convention being hosted there added a secure touch.

The people I encountered along the way spit out directions with confident authority. I couldn't be mad at them. Their intentions were good, though they still left me to a wild goose chase. First left, then right; forward, then backwards. With each wrong turn my urgency increased, the pressure within kept building.

I was so close, literally, to not holding it when a sympathetic employee guided me to the promised land deep within an obscure corner of the basement where I took care of business. Free at last, free at last.

Finding an electrical outlet at a coffee shop sometimes descends into outright competitive warfare with other laptop users. It's a basic matter of supply and demand. We all eye the plugged-in user like a hawk, silently developing our strategy while scoping out the competition. Each man for himself. The second someone unplugs, we pounce. Hesitate for a second and the enemy wins.

The smart combatant takes note of clues and readies a preemptive strike. A plugged-in user about to unplug decreases the time he spends staring at his screen by a perceptible amount. By the same token, he increases the frequency of checking his backpack for something he thinks is in there. His focus wanes. His body form changes. It's not as rigid as it used to be. The curve in his back becomes more perpendicular. He starts rubbing his neck. The ability to recognize these warning signs is a fine art, and I have plenty of veteran experience.

On this day, as luck would have it, there were no competitors in sight, but another problem arose instead. Those darn coffee shops tend to hide those outlets and it takes Sherlock Holmes to find them. Persistent, sleuth-like, I found one.

I opened the laptop, clicked on the word processor, and fired up my optimism. I plunked down a few words for my daily journal. That's it. I frittered away the next chunk of time by flipping through the pages of *Tried by War: Lincoln as Commander in Chief*.

Surfing the internet proved to be the highlight of the afternoon. I solved unanswered questions about Bogart's: the Big Guy manning the front door at Bogart's is the brains behind the ribs at Pappy's, Skip Steele; he's their Master Chef. What's he doing at Bogart's? Well, he's the Master Chef there, too.

That orange sauce with the slightly spicy kick is an apricot sauce with a sprinkle of black pepper. The Big Guy's final act of culinary glory is to blowtorch the ribs after he applies the apricot rub.

Curiosity kept gnawing at me about burnt ends. They didn't sound yummy, and besides, what are they? The answer lay only a few keystrokes away:

from (pelletenvy.blogspot.com)

People have so many questions about burnt ends. What are they? How do you make them? If they're burnt, how can they be good? Well, let me tell you that burnt ends are a Kansas City thang. Barbeque joints in other parts of the country may offer them now, but to my knowledge, they started right here in KC.

Charlie Bryant bought out Henry Perry, our first barbeque entrepreneur of record, who served barbeque out of a barn near 17th & Highland in Kansas City starting in 1908. Arthur Bryant took over for his older brother some years later and moved the business to 18th & Brooklyn, just a few blocks from the old Municipal Stadium. That stadium was the home of the Kansas City Blues and later, the Kansas City A's. It was also the first home of the Kansas City Chiefs. Being so close to the stadium, Arthur Bryant's reputation for barbeque grew magnificently.

The restaurant started out organized cafeteria style, as it still is all these years later. Customers would wait in line to order, then take their food on a tray to an available seat. While waiting in line, folks could snatch a handful of chopped up, well cooked ends of the briskets that had been sliced to order. These morsels were soon to be coined "burnt ends." Over time, the burnt ends became so popular, Arthur Bryant decided this meat, previously thought of as scrap or waste, had value and began charging customers for their crunchy, savory fix. Rumor has it that this didn't set well at first. Despite opposition from the regulars, the trend caught on in Kansas City.

These days, to meet demand, cuts of meat are sacrificed specifically to create burnt ends. Additionally, any over cooked piece of meat chopped into an unrecognizable form, be it beef, pork or otherwise, is now labeled as burnt ends and served, usually swimming in sauce.

However, in traditional barbeque establishments, in addition to the over cooked parts and pieces left after slicing, brisket points are the acceptable cut of meat to create burnt ends. Whole briskets are cooked, the leaner flats are separated and sliced, while the fattier points return to the pit to further render their additional internal fat. The points exit the pit very dark, in an almost meteorite like state, with a smoky, crispy exterior wonderfully balanced by a moist, tender interior. They are cubed up and served as an entree or on bread or bun as a sandwich. When they're good, they're awesome. In fact, they're almost indescribably the best barbeque under the sun. Big statement I know, but when was the last time you had great burnt ends? I rest my case ... Oh, and those of you drooling on the keyboards, I know you're gettin' this!

Reading *Tried by War: Lincoln as Commander in Chief* and surfing the internet chewed up the clock. And Panic set in leading me to enact a two-minute drill. The clock on the wall read 5:30 pm. The game started at 6:15 pm. Anxieties were on the rise.

An unfilled promise I had made to myself remained. I needed to seek out the public library and give them a plug for my business book. I had been successful in Dwight; who's to say I wouldn't be successful again? In the course of the day this got rationalized away with a litany of excuses: *Oh it is so hot; I really need to find Bogart's; I'll just bike around a little longer and find a*

Starbucks; the library probably closes early on Saturdays; it is getting late; it is probably hard to find, etc. It would have taken very little effort to accomplish this simple task, but lame and lazy joined the party.

Heading south from Starbucks my pedals spun faster than a windmill in a hurricane. Up ahead, high above the doorway, chiseled letters read, PUBLIC LIBRARY. The lights were on, but I used a final act of rationalization, *I don't want to be late for the game*, and hammered on past.

But my Catholic side took over, releasing the floodwaters of shame and guilt. It would've taken only five or ten minutes to stop and ask, but my rationalization process defeated that like Napoleon at Waterloo. In order to properly assuage the guilt gods, I determined I'd need to call back down to St. Louis upon my return to Minneapolis. The clouds of shame and guilt hung in the air for weeks. There wasn't an easy way to delete them except to make the call. I never did.

* * *

Since I wasn't wearing socks, my feet hurt something terrible from the blisters. I had no one to blame but myself. A small urban park with an inviting water fountain sat a couple of blocks from the stadium. I waged an internal debate to do it or not.

Off came my shoes exposing blisters. I crawled on the curved, slippery fountain edge, sliding my feet in the water. It felt cool and soothing. Fall in and I'm a fool.

I finally scampered over to the game where the stadium stood tall and proud. The anticipation of seeing the Cardinals ripped at my stomach. Reaching the seat listed on my ticket took a series of escalator rides up and up and up and up. Way up on the 4th deck behind home plate.

The panoramic view of the St. Louis skyline can only be described as National Geographic quality. The architects had obviously spent an unconscionable amount of time placing the stadium in the perfect position so fans would have the most perfect, most glorious view of the Arch. I stood with pride during the *Star Spangled Banner* and sat down ready for the ballgame to begin.

There isn't a simple way to exaggerate the cosmic distance of my seat. Hitching a ride on a hot air balloon stood among the better options for getting back down to Mother Earth, with the movie *The Air Up There* a visual model of success. The players were pin-size dots on a small patch of green far below. Only astronauts are this high up, I thought.

There are few things greater in life than soaking in a baseball game on a clear lazy evening with only the *whack* of the bat interrupting the collective serenity. The dense array of retina pleasure, from the lush green grass to the collage of colors enveloping the stadium, arouses a visual feast unmatched anywhere. People are happy, smells of tasty cuisine rise through the air, and the festive atmosphere spreads good cheer throughout the soul.

Hunger pangs multiplied as the game progressed. In today's competitive marketplace, teams have transformed concessions stands from dinky little kiosks serving minimal baseball fare into centers of exotic cuisine.

Taking the stairs down to an open air marketplace resulted in being confronted with a sea of red baseball hats. This is like an urban village, I thought. Shops and stands lined the concourse while people zoomed and crashed like bumper cars at the State Fair.

At one concession stand lines screamed five across, ten deep. The engineer in me concocted an algorithm to get to the front in the shortest possible time. Monitoring the lines, if one shortened, even a little, I made an automatic jump. My algorithm demanded a repeat of this process until I achieved victory. All I ended up really doing was bouncing from one line to another. I didn't save time at all. In fact, I lost time. My algorithm had failed, and failed badly.

Exotic food choices made decision-making impossible. Regular hot dog or jumbo hot dog? Bratzel dog or Pretzel dog? Skip all of them and instead go with Polish sausage? Nachos? Nachos supreme? Or Nachos grande with pulled pork? Chicken tenders, beef brisket, turkey leg, or BBQ pulled pork sandwich? Sides of freshly-made coleslaw, baked beans, or French fries? Toppings of Cheese cup, sour cream, potato chip, Cracker Jacks, popcorn or licorice? For dessert should I go with a malt cup, Cardinals ice cream bar or Rich'n Chip? Regular Coke or souvenir Coke? In the end, safe and conservative won the day. A regular Coke, hot dog, and a malt cup.

The spacious concourse had moms and dads traipsing in all directions with their kids in tow barking orders at them: "Mommy, I want a pop. Daddy, get me an ice cream. Mommy, I'm hungry. Daddy, I want a hotdog. Mommy, daddy I have to go to the bathroom."

Parents proved themselves to be highly skilled magicians as they held a Coke in one hand while they squeezed hotdogs in the other, all while chasing after their kids. A traffic jam circled the condiment counters with hands squirting gobs of ketchup and mustard on everything possible. Kids had ketchup smeared on one side of their chins while chocolate coated the other. The ball game faded into the background.

Whole families were the most amusing. They exited the souvenir shop with each member wearing a jersey with the name of their favorite player on the back. The kids made out like bandits. Besides scoring jerseys, they scored baseball hats and mini-Louisville sluggers to boot. The dads frowned a lot.

Eventually my soul found its way back to the seat.

While I savored being in the moment, a man emerged from the walkway during the 5th inning; blue t-shirt, sunglasses, baseball hat turned backwards, and clutching a beer. He gazed for a long time at the playing field far below. Turning, he faced the steep stairs he was about to climb, contemplating for a long time. His body language confirmed what everyone in our section knew.

"What the (*bleep*)" he said. The final word came out very slow.

The gentleman next to me looked at him and said, "Did you bring an extra oxygen tank with you?" All of us sitting nearby smirked.

The man in the blue t-shirt and baseball hat turned backward stared upward again. "(*Bleep*)" came out again, very slow, for the second time in less than a minute. Staring for a final moment, he lowered his head and took the first step.

I read an article in the Minneapolis StarTribune where the architect who designed Target Field said that on average he has 12 acres to work with when designing a baseball stadium. But in the case of Target Field itself he had only 8 acres to work with. The problem was that the land it sits on, formerly a parking lot, is constrained on one side by a county incinerator and on the other side by Target Center, home of the Minnesota Timberwolves.

Busch stadium, on the other hand, sits on at least 12 acres. The meticulous, detail seeking perfectionist qualities I have couldn't accept that Busch stadium sits on *at least* 12 acres. Too vague and imprecise. To rectify this lack of clarity, later, I sat on my laptop sifting through every available online document much like Colombo, the famous TV detective. I searched, digged, and clawed for that elusive, mysterious exact figure. I came up donuts. Somewhere someone, perhaps a real estate agent or tax collector, knew that number. It just wasn't me.

In Target Field, the fans are eyeball close to the field, but a pair of binoculars would help in Busch Stadium.

There is no open air concourse at Target Field, no room. Busch Stadium, though, has the greatest, most fun open air concourse anywhere.

Target Field holds 39,000 while Busch stadium holds 47,000. Target Field is built from Minnesota limestone giving it a very light brown sandy look. In contrast, Busch Stadium is made from dark colonial brownstone brick. Both are built on the edge of their respective downtowns and close to the Mississippi River.

The whole game the Cardinals would fall behind, then catch up, then fall behind, then catch up again. In the 8th inning the Red Birds caught up and moved ahead to stay. They won the game 5-4, breaking a 7-game losing streak. My boyhood hero, the legend himself, Lou Brock, attended the game. Happy Birthday, Lou.

Now that the game was over, several options presented themselves. Option one: leaving early the next morning, which would mean driving over 700 miles in one day. Option two: skipping Kansas City and leaving straight from St. Louis, which would mean skipping the barbeque center of the Universe! Option three: a cool refreshing shower, which offered the most appeal.

The game ended around 9 pm and getting back to the campground in Cahokia took the usual few minutes. I passed those seductive naughty bars again. And those generously rotund gentlemen still worked their smokers. Billows of smoke drifted high in the air as the sweet smell of barbeque invaded my senses, again. Temptation persisted and, like before, lust followed close behind.

Driving towards Kansas City now offered the greatest chance of success. Passing Lambert International airport led to reflection because it only took twenty minutes to get there from Cahokia. A few nights earlier the Erio's Pizza employee made it sound like they was on the far side of the moon. According to her, getting there wasn't doable in an hour and forty-five minutes. I seethed and ground my teeth just thinking about this. But with St.

Louis in the rear view mirror, I focused on the road ahead.

When sleepiness sets in, it means it's time to pull over. No exceptions. I don't want to be a news story about a guy falling asleep and crashing into a tree doing 75. Just a little further, just a little further, I kept thinking. But when an angry army of lightning bolts ripped across the sky with a take-no-prisoners attitude, I wasted no time in careening my Ford Focus straight to the exit.

It was now 3 am. The sign on the front of the motel office said, PUSH THE BUTTON, so I pushed the button. The clerk, a native of India, had the patience of an angel. Either that or she was a good actor.

"I'm on a barbeque tour in search for the perfect barbeque," I said. She nodded and smiled.

"I've traveled to India before. I want to go back." She nodded and smiled at that, too.

"Do you know I am paying less for this motel room than for a campground?" She looked at me, nodded, and smiled.

"It's really bad out. I pulled over after seeing a bunch of lightning bolts rip across the sky. I got spooked."

Her eyes got bigger and she nodded a final time, but didn't smile. "Oh my goodness, I got spooked, too," she said, "I saw them and they scared me. Here's your room key."

CHAPTER 7

imagine that

Legendary coaches have great game plans to spur their teams to victory. Today, my game plan would be to get up early, book it to Kansas City, eat ribs, check out downtown, and leave for Minneapolis by noon. In my idealistic brain this seemed doable.

The alarm went off at 8:30 am as planned. Every now and then I have resentments over the intrusion that technology represents. I once drove a minivan over a pager to cure myself of this. It was the most freeing thing I have ever done. A lifelong dream has been to take a sledge hammer to the alarm clock when it goes off. Would today be that day?

The phone rang at precisely 11 am with a polite reminder that it was checkout time and that I should please get lost. I threw my stuff in the car and drove over to the motel office.

Along the way I encountered the Indian lady walking across the parking lot. I said to her, "I left my key in the room."

"Oh. Thank you," she said. We breezed through exotic topics like the storm the night before, the sunny day, and how far it was to Minneapolis. I held out hope that she had a beautiful daughter back in India dying to meet me. It didn't happen.

My car, too, had problems with getup and go. It would run rough and cut out. This same problem occurred a year ago on my way back from Chicago. It had something to do with the gas. Back then I continued to drive, but with a quick flick of the wrist turn the ignition key off and then back on. This time my technique failed. It took a couple more tries before it worked, but the car still had a jerky motion.

Cruising down I-70 towards Kansas City there wasn't a convenient way to avoid the alluring glare of the big bright yellow banner that read DOUBLE J's BBQ RANCH in big bold red letters. Hallelujah! Breakfast time.

The interior looked like a ranch house, incorporating moose antlers, cowboy pictures and plain tan colors. A cheery waitress guided me to a booth. A group of senior citizens occupied the center tables.

The black t-shirt the waitress wore stood out. It had a colorful orange design with LED ZEPPELIN spelled out in large yellow letters outlined in black.

Like the waitress in Springfield she was camera shy. Greedy for more video, I reasoned that bragging about other great ribs on my search might motivate her, driving her to a spirit of competition and forcing her hand to help me out; I even boasted about Mark Feed's Store in Louisville.

Out of nowhere she got a dose of bravery, saying for the camera, "Hi from Double J's BBQ Ranch in New Florence, Missouri."

I moved in for the kill, asking, "Are these St. Louis-style ribs? Or Memphis-style ribs?"

"Neither. They're Kansas City-style ribs." According to her, "The cook makes them based on what he learned while in Kansas City. Therefore, they are Kansas City-style ribs."

Kansas City-style ribs? Wasn't the world of barbeque split into only two camps? St. Louis-style ribs and Memphis-style ribs? Now there's a third?

"People who make barbeque ribs have big egos, don't they?" I said.

"Yeah, when it comes to ribs, egos are huge," she said, rolling her eyes and flashing a short smile. She left to serve the senior citizens.

My ribs showed up and they weren't about to get a free pass just because they were Kansas City-style ribs. I peered, scrutinized, and analyzed. They had a high bar to meet.

The beans and applesauce were average at best. They were nothing to write home to mom about. The ribs, however, were a different story. The good size half-slab was wide and thick, running the length of the plate and possessing a nice muddy brown color. The barbeque aroma had an awe-inducing brown sugar scent that brought stillness to the day. For a nice touch they served Texas toast, the only place on the tour to do so.

A defining characteristic of barbeque ribs is the rate of speed by which the meat comes off the bones. If I have to rip and tear using all the muscles in my jaw bone, the rate of speed is too slow. If the meat slides off too easily, not giving me a chance to bite and chew and savor the joy, the rate of speed is too fast.

But these ribs had the perfect rate of speed; I didn't have to rip and tear, yet I was able to bite and chew with delight, allowing the smooth tasty morsels to slide down my throat with ease. The tongue took delight as the soft texture of each morsel tickled it on the way down. Kansas City-style rub has a sweet sugar cane sensation from the molasses in it. My exploding taste buds took note.

The sauce had no hint of bitterness. Instead, it had the right blend of sweet. Too much sweet and it tastes like sugar on steroids. Too little sweet and it tastes like flavored water. No, the chef created the perfect blend. Just like Sander's Hot Fudge transforms the mundane task of eating vanilla ice cream into an out of body experience, so did the sauce in transforming these ribs.

My Grandma never made barbeque ribs, but she always had the magic touch. When she made burgers they always tasted better than anyone else's. The Old Dutch potato chips she served tasted better too. Double J's had the same magic touch my Grandma had.

So far on my tour they had the best overall ribs. Palatably the right combination of ribs, rub, and sauce. The whole was greater than the sum of its parts. This might sound like Einstein's theory on barbeque, but it's the plain, simple, honest, unvarnished truth.

Straight to the point, Double J's wasn't one of the Big Three in Kansas City. They were more like Joe Montana, the former NFL quarterback. He got drafted low with no expectations, but went on to a Hall of Fame career winning four Super Bowls.

Between the booth and cash register the waitress lost her camera shyness. She said, "I've always been told that barbeque originated in Kansas City, that it's the best, and that's what we fashion our barbeque after. And then if you head up the highway and go about 120 miles on 70 west, at the Concordia exit, get off and go left across the overpass, there's Biffle's Barbeque. They have ribs and stuff like that, but it's more of a sandwich thing. They're awesome. Not as good as us, but they're good."

During this conversation her simple facial movements twisted and contorted in ways I couldn't keep up with. Engaged in deep thought at times, her face squished and squeezed like Popeye, the cartoon character. At other times she broke into oversized grins. With alarming frequency her right hand flung perpendicular to the right while her left hand moved as quick as a blur.

"You blubbered about Arthur Bryant's in Kansas City?"

"Oh they're excellent, they're awesome, they're really good. They have a reputation. I saw them on the Food Channel. They were talking about barbeque places and named their top ten in the nation and Arthur Bryant's was one of them."

"Holy buckets, Arthur Bryant's it is then." My new itinerary had me in Kansas City at 3 pm. Any thoughts of meeting Tami the Trucker along the way were forgotten.

In a twist of irony, reading *Churchill* gained significance 30 miles west of New Florence. At Westminster College in the tiny city of Fulton, Missouri, Winston Churchill made his famous Iron Curtain Speech on March 5, 1946. The National Churchill Museum is located on campus, a bare stone's throw from I-70. But being in a hurry, I didn't stop.

As a young man in Britain, Winston Churchill grew up in a powerful political family. Groomed by his mother, he used his early military career to boost his name recognition back home, aided by writing vivid battlefront articles for British newspapers.

Upon entering politics he became instrumental in Britain's command of World War I. Blamed and demonized for military decisions gone bad, he got voted out of office. Clawing his way back into politics, years later, he made it into Parliament. He rose to the position of Prime Minister during World War II and guided Britain during its darkest hour. Upon war's end he was unceremoniously dumped by the voters.

Beset by financial ruin in the stock market crash of 1929 (his broker bought stocks for him on margin) Churchill rose from the abyss through his writing. Sadly, stock market reverses ruined him again in the late 1930s. But once more his writing nursed him back to financial health.

He never believed in spending less when his goal was to increase his lifestyle. Instead, he made more money to match his ambitions. Over his lifetime he authored 43 books. He died at the ripe old age of 95 still involved in politics.

Not far down the road, approaching Kansas City, signs tempted innocent tourists into visiting the Presidential Library of their native son, Harry S. Truman, who was joined at the political hip during World War II to Winston Churchill.

Exiting at Independence, I waged a fierce internal debate over the remote possibility of missing Arthur

Bryant's. I confronted this dilemma from a left turn lane and decided that Harry S. Truman should take a backseat to Arthur Bryant. But not before driving a stake in the hearts of fellow motorists by spurting into oncoming traffic from an ignorant lack of attention.

At a gas station off the freeway, a technology hero pulled out her Smartphone and pulled up a map. It wasn't perfect, but it got me to the original Arthur Bryant's on 18th and Brooklyn. The neighborhood had an eerie feel to it, though it wasn't anything specific that led me to feel this way.

Parking on the street one couldn't help but notice the huge Arthur Bryant's sign painted on the side of the two-story brown brick building. An inviting aroma arrested my soul well before I grabbed the door handle. The interior looked more like a small town family cafeteria. The menu, extending from window 1 to window 3, made ordering easy.

"Literally everywhere I go everyone keeps telling me about Arthur Bryant's," I told the gentleman in front of me in line.

He shook his head, grinning, "I drove over 30 miles just to pick up barbeque sandwiches. I know what you're talking about." It took his patient help for it to register that long ribs meant St. Louis-style ribs and short ribs meant Baby Back ribs.

Finally reaching the front of the line, I said, "I would like the short ribs, baked beans and fries."

"Would you like anything to drink?" the cashier asked.

"Give me a Diet Coke too." I found a table, sat down, and looked up. I noticed an older gentleman, a man of mystery with an outlaw grin peering at me.

Seeing a worker nearby and always in search of the next great interview, I announced to the worker, "I'm on a barbeque tour and I am trying to interview someone everywhere I go. Are you camera shy?" He ignored me.

Seeing another worker, I proclaimed, "I'm on a bar-beque tour and I'm trying to interview someone every-where I go. You're not camera shy, are you?"

"Not a chance buddy." He didn't try to fake his rude attitude. An uneasy silence ensued. At random he said, "Follow me." We marched towards the kitchen and he told everyone in our path, "This guy is on a barbeque tour and wants to take pictures." Once inside the kitchen, he said, "Go ahead, snap away."

"Is it ok if I get a close up of the smoker? Is anyone camera shy here? Do they mind if I take their pictures?"

"You can shoot anything you want. Go ahead."

I had to work overtime to contain myself as I didn't want my giddiness to blow the opportunity. Workers, a lot of old timers, originals from the early decades of Arthur Bryant's, crowded about doing every job imagin-able. I was shocked at the small confined kitchen space because most commercial kitchens have at least some size to them. This was more like an oversized closet. Em-ployees crashed into each other like bumper cars, leading me to wonder on how they got anything done without getting hurt.

Despite the crammed space, the crew operated like a well oiled machine. Never was there a moment when the *whack, whack, whack* of the hatchet sized knives chop-ping slabs didn't fill the room.

Navigating over to the smoker, the centerpiece of the kitchen, wasn't easy. First I made a casual left around the soda machine, then contortions along a curvy path sneaking by the French fry cooker, followed by a sharp right around the chopping cart. I had to compress into the work space between the serving counter and smoker. I had no choice but to rotate sideways. Once there, an 180 degree flip had me facing the cast iron doors protect-ing the slabs inside.

The smoker is really an oversized wood-burning fur-nace that had gotten a lot of use over the years. The black mortar that held the white bricks together was rough and uneven. In modern construction, the mortar holding the bricks together is even and smooth.

Oh my God, I thought. I'm staring into a dark celestial space the size of an underground cave, filled with more slabs than I could eat in a lifetime. The very essence and soul of barbeque is 12 inches away. Fame and fortune is won or lost based on the secrets locked within. I'm standing at the very door of history!

I could see nothing but luxurious brown. Whole pork painted the top rack and filled every available space, like a gorgeous Van Gogh painting fills a canvas that leaves art lovers breathless. I had a strong impulse to reach out and grab one. It took a mountain of courage to not do it.

Slabs of ribs graced the lower rack. Dark brown, tempting and gorgeous, they filled every nook and cranny. Not just filled, *filled*. An extra deep breath filled my lungs with as much aroma as they desired. Slab upon slab upon slab, a universe of slabs. Can the rack even hold that much weight? It would take a forklift to load all of that. Drifting, billowing smoke further stroked the luxurious brown.

Back at the table I lined up sauces behind my plate of ribs. I took the bottle of SWEET and squeezed with all my might, covering the ribs in an ocean of reddish brown glory. Not stopping there, I grabbed the ORIGINAL, and added extra layers of goo for a finishing touch. I had so much sauce slathered on them I couldn't see even a tiny nib of meat underneath.

The problem was that I didn't quite read every detail on the labels. The SWEET sauce was sweet *and* spicy. The ORIGINAL was tangy *times* two. Oops. When I took a bite I got met with bitter taste. Blast it. I hate spicy. Why, oh why did I do that? Hindsight is 20/20. I pretended it didn't matter and took another bite. More bitterness. I began to engage in delusional rationalization:

These ribs aren't as good as others I've tasted, too spicy, the meat isn't all that tender, kind of tough.

The liar in me couldn't keep a straight face. A feeling of failure, dejection and regret rushed in. All the build-up, all the talking, all the recommendations, all the anticipation—the reputation that preceded itself. All of it blown by a couple of impatient squirts. The man of mystery with the outlaw grin kept a watchful eye, never taking his eyes off me.

A nearby employee said, "You have sauce on your face, sir." I had no reason to doubt him.

Pulling out my camera, I asked the man of mystery, "Do I really have sauce all over my face?"

"No," he said, as he got up to leave. Passing by the table he stopped, looked, and said, "Clean the meat off those bones," adding an extra dose of outlaw to his grin.

Looking down, my spirits lifted. Buried amongst the bones, ready for action, was reddish meat devoid of any sauce. It laid patient and still, waiting to be devoured. When I looked up, the man of mystery had vanished.

I dug in like a piranha and had those bones bare in seconds. I'm sure those around me thought I ate like a pig. The raw smokey power of the meat tasted off the charts, no longer tainted by the slathering sauces. No finesse, no sophistication. Just pure, raw, unadulterated power.

The afternoon wound down and the time to leave had come. Outside, I had one more thing to do. Give any of us the smallest opportunity with a camera and we turn into National Geographic photographer wannabes.

I worked and fidgeted in trying to get the yellow Coke cup to sit on my car trunk in perfect alignment with the Arthur Bryant's sign painted on the building so I could get the perfect picture. This proved to be elusive. More fidgeting, more fussing. At long last, the stars aligned and I finally got it right. Snapping for a final time

I looked into the camera and said, "The Mr. Y. BBQ Tour is now officially over."

Time to step on the gas and get back to Minneapolis. Or was it? I made a spontaneous decision to visit the Harry S. Truman Library in Independence, only five minutes away. I didn't want the sour taste of regret to taint a one-of-a-kind trip.

Everything in Independence is named after Truman; the roads, buildings, and squares. Everything. The Harry S. Truman Presidential Library, a large white stone building, settles on a gentle sloping hill.

The history buff in me wanted to explore every inch, but a problem came to light. It was 4:30 pm and they closed at 5:00 pm. It's hard to rationalize paying $7 for half an hour; I would barely have time for cursory looks. Instead I cruised the couple of steps back out front, hit the record button and said, "Hi from the Harry S. Truman Presidential Library," then left.

Road Construction in Missouri is nothing like road construction in Illinois, I thought, bolting home on I-35 north to Minneapolis. If not for the orange cones no one would notice.

The blistering heat made life unbearable. Up went the windows and on went the air conditioner. Did you know you save more gas by driving with the windows up and the air conditioning on? Yep, less drag and turbulence. Cooler, too.

The Missouri countryside breezed by. Needing gas, I exited at New Hampton, 21 miles before the Iowa border. Pulling into the station, a white Chevy SUV sat parked on the grassy edge of the lot. Attached to it was a large barbeque smoker with billowing white smoke drifting skyward. Go figure. A slim, athletic, Hawaiian looking gentleman wearing a baseball hat manned it.

Scrambling to pull out the camera, I said, "The Mr. Y. BBQ Tour hasn't ended yet after all, I thought it did in Kansas City."

"Bear's Aloha Grill, New Hampton, Missouri. Google search it," the gentleman said terse, working the smoker fast and furious; keeping up became impossible. In another life he might have been a juggler. He wasted no time in preparing a plate.

"I'm Tim. What's your name?"

"Barry, but my friends call me Bear. Bear's Aloha Grill."

Bear, I discovered, is a natural schmoozer. We chatted for at least 40 minutes and left no topic untouched. After moving my car we talked some more. If the need to get back to Minneapolis didn't exist we would've schmoozed until the sun went down and came back up again the next day.

At its core, Bear's story is an adventure. He is a unique blend of carpe diem and opportunistic optimism. The world needed to know more about him.

I got my camera rolling: "I'm Barry Williams from Bear's Aloha Grill. I started out at the Four Seasons in Chicago, a very high-profile kitchen. I was transferred to Four Seasons in Maui, Hawaii, and opened my own restaurant there, The PuPu Lounge Seafood and Grill. Hawaiian PuPu cuisine is my specialty."

I looked it up. PuPu is another name for Hawaiian appetizers. This became popular in the 1940s, fusing Polynesian, Cantonese, and Hawaiian cooking. It includes cubed seasoned fish, spareribs, wontons, tempura vegetables, chicken, and egg rolls.

When Bear speaks he doesn't say his words with monotone fact. He spins them with shameless huckster-ism, leaving listeners with the hidden sales pitch of a car salesman, yet, the qualities of honor and respect blend, swirl, and mix to form the utmost in professionalism. Courteous and polite, Bear is likable three steps beyond Tuesday.

"Do you set up here all the time?"

"As much as I can." Bear kept piling food on my plate.

"What am I looking at here?"

"You're looking at Bear's Aloha Grill's smoked pork picnic ham." The smells and colors melded, creating desperation out of hunger, even though I'd eaten my fill mere hours before.

"How did you get interested in barbeque?"

"Growing up I always liked barbeque and became very interested in it. As I got older I just kept working at it."

He'd gone through a divorce a year earlier. "I'm still affected by it," he said. I could feel the emotional toll it took on him, especially when he described the consequences of it. "I've put my hay farm up for sale and at some point I'll probably put the restaurant up for sale, too." He is a deeply spiritual man and practices the oldest, purest kind of Yoga.

As I stood there, a stream of friends and customers stopped by. He introduced me to each of them with, "This is Tim from Minneapolis. He's on a barbeque tour. This is his third barbeque today." It always took a while before their collective laughs died down.

Fumbling with my camera, I said, "Oh, I'm on, give me a run down on what I'm looking at here."

"Thank you so much. This is my smoked brisket with potato mac salad. It's my own recipe. Fresh-roasted corn on the cob from my smoker. A beautiful bone-in picnic ham and my Bear's Aloha Grill BBQ sauce."

"Go ahead. Slather the sauce on. Is your sauce sweet or tangy? Or somewhere in between?"

"Somewhere in between."

He used a special Himalayan salt on the corn. It had every vitamin a human could ever need in the course of a day. A bottle of water and dinner roll were thrown in to boot.

My plate overflowed. I didn't see how I could finish

imagine that

it. No way. The aroma, texture, color, and flavor of each item synthesized together in a beautiful symphony with Bear as the conductor. Each food played an important role in this concerto and the distinctions between them blurred, every bite devoured in reverent, spiritual bliss. I became desperate for more picnic ham (how I had room I don't know). I can't explain it, but a rare loss of words interfered.

In the midst of my gorging I couldn't forget my friends. "Alright Sandifer, alright McCoy," I said, facing Minneapolis. "You thought I was done eating, but I am the King." Bear ran the camera, "I'm not done, check this out, I hope you're jealous. I hope you're really, really jealous." I took an extra large bite out of the corn on the cob just for them.

Bear couldn't believe I'd finished the whole plate. Neither could I.

I probed. "What's the secret to your barbeque?"

"I put the Aloha Spirit in everything I do."

"You gotta try his ribs, too," his friend Jeff said, hooking onto Bear's infectious persona.

"When I get them," Bear said.

"He's got great ribs."

"Thank you so much."

"It's just hard to beat a good barbeque rib," I said.

"There are good ones out there, but his, you eat them and you like them, and then after a while ...." Jeff said.

"Yeah, it becomes an addiction. It is. It is an addiction," I said, talking over him.

"His aren't greasy, they're real light."

"Thank you so much," Bear said.

Jeff, like all other barbeque addicts, waits for the right moment to share his favorite barbeque establishment. As though part of a 12-step program, it took an enabler like me to get him to unlock the secret within. "It's a different kind, from the Mid-South. They use cayenne pepper and vinegar. Only pork—you can't get beef there, just pork."

"It's on the border of Kentucky and Tennessee?" I asked.

"Yes, near the Tennessee, Kentucky border. Hopkinsville, Clarksville, Nashville." Being I had my face stuffed with food I didn't think to ask for the name of the place.

My internet research shows that Hopkinsville, Kentucky, and Nashville, Tennessee, are separated by 40 miles, with Clarksville, Tennessee, in the literal middle right along the Kentucky border. Between Hopkinsville and Clarksville alone there are 20 plus barbeque establishments, not to mention Nashville's. Curiosity killing the cat? Want to know what place he was talking about? Me too. I'll see you down there.

On a side note, in a few years a total eclipse of the sun will darken Hopkinsville for a longer period of time than anywhere else on the planet—2 minutes 40 seconds to be exact. Just an idea, but when it hits, you might want to visit Mike Mathis and his Wood Shed Bar-B-Q, only a few miles from the best spot on the planet for viewing the eclipse.

* * *

A person's I.Q. skyrockets a couple of points just by reading the historical markers dotting I-35 north through Iowa. The Covered Bridges of Madison County are a short distance from the freeway and the movie of the same name, starring Clint Eastwood and Meryl Streep, was based on these bridges. Iowa (surprise) has a dynamic Brickyard and Smokestack Heritage. John Wayne, the actor (the Duke), was born in Winterset.

Around midnight all the food eaten during the day

started causing me trouble. Despite the need to exit, procrastination took over and the next exit kept moving up one exit further until Mother Nature forced my hand, leaving me no choice. I exited at a truck stop named Boondocks, 30 miles from Mason City. The vast surrounding farmlands lay as flat and as void as the surface of the moon.

Leonardo Da Vinci said that we should be curious about everything. The motel there charged $44 for a single room, but an arresting $48 for a double. Strange that a couple is charged a paltry $4 more. Single people are taken advantage of everywhere. Will it ever end? No.

At another exit, following the sign that said, MOTEL 1 MILE, I drove as far as 5 miles, but nothing existed except dark empty farms.

Curious about rates at a Super 8 motel near Mason City I asked the clerk, "How much is a single room for the night?"

"A single room is $69.95 plus tax" the clerk answered.

Are you kidding me? That much for a single room at a Super 8?

"Wait, let me double check," he said, as I started pushing through the door. "Nope." He looked up. "It's still $69.95 plus tax." My body wanted to go into convulsions.

In Albert Lea, Minnesota, a mom and pop motel charged a more-than-reasonable $38 including tax. The owner laughed heartily upon hearing that campgrounds and other motels charged more because of higher gas prices. At 2 am my head landed with a soft purr upon the fluffy pillow.

Getting up three hours later at 5 am, eating, showering and getting on the Interstate, I experienced smooth sailing until approaching Burnsville Center, where a logic-defying traffic jam turned the freeway into a parking lot all the way to the Minnesota River. Was it road construction? Nope. An accident? Nope. A deer crossing the road? Nope. Did the road narrow? Nope. Not a single, simple reason for the jam could be found.

It took one hour to drive those last three miles. One hour. Traffic returned to normal after the single act of crossing the bridge, as though some kind of miracle healing had taken place. When I entered the school parking lot to report to work, the clock on my dash read 8 am, on the dot. You have to agree, timing *is* everything.

CHAPTER 8

i know what i did last summer

I never know what's going to happen over the months of summer. The dread of winter has ended, with its biting cold and lack of vitamin D. No longer do I have to get up and go to work in the dark, and when the day ends rush home in the monotony of darkness, again, to a bad dinner and depressing TV shows. I don't work out as much either. I gain weight and then complain about it to my co-workers at school.

But when spring hits and rolls into summer, optimism is in the air. All of us smile more and the sapping blahs are replenished by the pouncing sun, restoring the vitamin D we so desperately need. It's that period of year when the crack of the bats take root and bicycles are on the roll, gliding down bike trails and flying in chaos along urban streets.

It's also that time of year I make a grab for extra cash by working at the juvenile correctional facility, where I do my part to set the troubled youth of America on a new trajectory.

At lunch one day Mr. Seiwert, A.K.A. Sweet Lou, a co-worker, asked, "What did you do during your time off?"

"I went on a barbeque tour," I said.

My answer triggered a tidal wave. "Wow. Then you have to go to Rooster's. They're the best anywhere, bar none." Others at the table perked up and listened in to Sweet Lou.

"Where's Rooster's? I've never heard of them before," I said.

"Over in St. Paul. You have to go there. They are to die for. They are by far the best. I've eaten at a lot of places and nobody comes close. You gotta try them."

Mulling this over I asked, "Have you ever tried Big Daddy's in St. Paul? I think they are the best."

Sweet Lou said, "I've tried them all. Rooster's is better than anyone by a mile." There was no arguing the fact with him. He got me thinking.

Still questioning, I asked, "Have any of you ever been to Rudolph's BBQ?" Located in the Uptown area of Minneapolis, their reputation cuts a wide swath. "Sandifer and McCoy kept talking about them. They both say nobody is even close. I tried them, but didn't find them that good. Dry and flat. Not much meat on them either. I've heard others say they are the best, but they weren't that good for me."

"Rudolph's used to be the best, until they did their remodeling," Sweet Lou said.

The administrator sitting next to him agreed. "Ever since they did the remodel, they went downhill."

These conversations weren't limited to the lunchroom. Action Jackson passed me in the hallway one day as I headed out after work. Dressed in summer clothes, he wore a yellow shirt and light-colored pants. An African-American man, he is close to me in size and build. "Did you have any projects going this summer?" he asked.

"Yes, I went on the Mr. Y. BBQ Tour. All year long I heard from people at the other place about all these great barbeque places and I couldn't take it anymore. I went to Chicago, Springfield, St. Louis, and Kansas City. I wanted to go on a much bigger tour, but that is all I could do."

A county employee, he is known as Action Jackson for his intensity. He lowered his voice to a firm baritone and said, slowly, "I have a brother in California who

106

makes the most awesome ribs ever. He has his special sauce that's awesome. And when he cooks the ribs he turns them on all sides when grilling." His words, as forceful as steel, pierced like bullets. He stood closer, looking at me over the rim of his glasses, every muscle rigid, like a Drill Sergeant about to dress down a recruit. "My brother doesn't poke the ribs with a fork." He poked pretend ribs with an unseen fork. "That way all the juices stay in." His face, positioned inches from mine, froze me in place. I didn't dare move. "He pulls branches from his apple tree and places them in a square pattern on the grill." He yanked branches from a simulated tree, placing them in a square pattern around an imaginary grill. "When he's done, he cleans the grill with raw onions. Some Mexican people he knows told him that trick. Didn't know that, did you?" Pride shot from him like rays from the sun.

"I did not." I stood motionless for a moment, absorbing all he had told me. "You know," I said, "every time I mention barbeque to someone, something triggers in them. I can't explain it, but something sparks. I experience this everywhere I go."

He bore down on me with that Drill Sergeant stare of his, nodding in decided agreement. A smile escaped his lips, the first in our entire conversation, and he relaxed. "I know, it just happened in me," he said, his head shaking up and down in small happy movements.

* * *

Dialogues extended well beyond school borders. Lisa Ocone came to town from Indonesia, without warning. Her stay was short, but eventful. Her husband works for the State Department and because of this they move all over the world every two to three years. Before she had gotten married I visited her in Uzbekistan, and after she married I visited them in Poland, and again in Indonesia.

During my visit to Poland, she said, "I miss eating ribs in the United States. Everyone over here thinks their ribs are *sooo* great," using a mocking tone, "but they are nothing compared to the United States." Her voice reflected a rare sadness.

Her rib place of choice is Famous Dave's. In one of our many conversations during her stay here I asked if she had ever tried other rib places in the Twin Cities.

"I ate at some rib place in St. Paul a long time ago that was pretty good, but I don't remember the name."

I did. "That would be Old Kentucky BBQ at the Union Depot in St. Paul, right on the Mississippi River." I know because she went there with me. "Since you are in town you should expand your horizons a little and try some other places. There are so many here other than Famous Dave's. Maybe you'll find one you like better." It wasn't too hard to convince her.

I persuaded her to give Dickey's BBQ Pit in Burnsville a try. They are a privately-owned national barbeque chain that is expanding in Minnesota. I'm personally leery of big chains and not able to wrap my head around the idea that a chain cranking out massed produced ribs can compete with the love and care that only a mom and pop place can inject.

She shared a pulled pork sandwich with her little son, Evan. He was all smiles and she was, too. "This is pretty good," she said taking another bite. She's a picky eater, so her comment raised the bar on all other pulled pork. But that rare note of sadness appeared one more time. "I really miss the barbeque here in the States."

The ribs held their own and were tender enough. Not smokey like other places, but respectably good. The folks at Dickey's must be able to read minds because their sauce had a most pleasing sweetness about it.

Pay a little extra and buy a Coke in one of their big

yellow plastic cups, then remember to bring it back on future visits for free pop. Smart. The sides of baked beans and fries paralleled the ribs in being a respectable good.

What separates them from the crowd is their customer service. The online reviews talk about it and we experienced it. The employees, true to their reputation, came to our table ready to do whatever it took to make our experience a winning one. Normally this cannot be expected from a big chain, but credit to them, they do it, and do it well.

For me, Big Daddy's retained the title of Boss Hoss. For her, Famous Dave's still reigned. With pressure mounting to settle the debate, the next day we marched over to Famous Dave's with her dad.

Lisa Ocone liked what she was eating, in this case ribs, but had doubts. "I'm not so sure Famous Dave's is the best anymore. I'm so confused. But you have to agree they have great sides."

"Yes, they have great sides."

"Sides are really important."

"Yes, sides are important."

She continued. "I don't know any more if Famous Dave's is the best. I'm just not sure." Lisa Ocone left town a few days later with rather sudden speed.

I missed broadening her horizons, but since I was on a roll, Rack Shack BBQ harkened a few miles down the road from Dickey's.

They know how to connect with their customers, too. From stainless steel tables, a big easy-to-read menu, and their veritable array of regional sauces, they connect with the customer. Clean and organized, even their uniforms are integrated into a central theme. They've worked through their marketing strategy with a fine tooth comb, and it's working. For them the Einstein Theory applies: the whole is greater than the sum of the parts.

My half-slab of choice? St. Louis cut pork ribs. They offered a variety of sides, offering mac-and-cheese, beans, coleslaw, and corn bread, with other creative sides like Tater Salad, Smoked potato, and Corn Bake. Their food matched the down-home Texas, family atmosphere they created.

Yet, I thought their ribs were on the dryer side, tougher too, and I couldn't find a justification for their higher prices. Higher than any other place, and in my opinion, a glaring weakness. Competition in the world of barbeque is fierce. Competitors like Dickey's, a few miles away, stand ready to pounce.

As far as the sauces go, they were great joy. They offered sauces from all the major barbeque hot spots in the country: Carolina sauce, Houston sauce, Savannah sauce, Georgia Sauce, Kansas City sauce, Memphis sauce, Kentucky sauce, and St. Paulie sauce.

Given all the choices, a mental struggle emerged. No sense in making it hard. Georgia sauce on one rib, Memphis sauce on another, Savannah on another, and so on, ending with St. Paulie sauce poured on the last rib.

Each had their own special bite, and none stood out as being 100% sweet. Georgia sauce was the sweetest of the bunch. Not to worry. None of them were too tangy or spicy either. Beautiful. I took a risk and tried them all. It made my day.

Every aspect of Rack Shack BBQ played to a Texas theme. I can't prove that they originated from Texas. There's only ancillary evidence. For example, the ribs don't come on a plate; they come in a pan, a rather large one. The portions don't come small, they come large. But remember, their prices come large too. Everything is large in Texas.

* * *

For weeks after that school lunchtime conversation

Rooster's occupied a lot of space in my brain. Haunting me, the thoughts wouldn't leave. Pressure within built, like water behind a dam. Over time I perused their website and recruited others to go with me, but there always seemed to be some reason why they couldn't. But on this day, with free time and not willing to wait any longer, the dam burst.

Rooster's is easy to find—35E north towards downtown St. Paul, exit at Randolph, turn right, and drive a quarter of a mile to the corner of Randolph and Chatsworth.

Housed in a small brick building in a quaint little neighborhood, a big yellow sign with the name ROOSTER'S in red letters is plastered at the top of the building. They made an impression before I even stepped foot in the door; a sticker announced they were a member of the Kansas City Barbeque Association.

Jammed into a hole-in-the-wall space, the place was clean and bright. To the left, next to the counter, a cooler held pop and other drinks. Two small round tables dominated the center.

The menu covered the back wall like wrapping paper, extending from one end to the other. Two red-colored booths sat in silence underneath. And two small red park bench-like chairs butted up against the window facing the street, adding to the red theme. When sitting on them, customers would put the two round tables together to set their food on them. Two booths, two chairs, and two tables, just like their website says.

Impressive awards decorated the walls: Round-shaped awards. Square-shaped awards. Circle-shaped awards. Best-of-the-Twin-Cities awards. Best Memphis-style Ribs awards. Awards I'd never heard of before. Amongst them, hiding, a colorful hand-drawn rooster.

It must be an obligatory feature of a barbeque establishment for the kitchen to be crunched, cluttered, and worn out from use on a daily basis. Employees exhibited behavior that I'd witnessed at other barbeque establishments. They crashed into each other like bumper cars.

Sitting above the stove were a row of figurines including a pig, a rabbit, and a duck. Hidden among them was a cartoon drawing of two roosters. I identified this as the most unique detail.

The clerk working the counter, a thin 6' 2", agreed to be interviewed. Wearing a black Rooster's t-shirt, he donned a black Viking's hat, sporting a beard below a look that said he was all business.

Pulling out my camera, I spoke, "I'm inside Rooster's here in St. Paul and I'm going to say hi to the employee here," turning towards him.

"What do you want me to say?" he asked.

"Just say, you know, why Rooster's is the best, and ...."

Abruptly and without warning he pointed his left thumb at the guy to his left, and said terse, "Talk to him." I didn't process this well, standing there stuck and confused.

The guy he pointed to looked to be in his mid-forties and similar to me in size and build, his light brown hair sticking in a couple of directions, with a matching mustache to boot. On this hot blistering summer day, the fast and furious pace he worked at left sweat dripping down his face in a steady stream with sweat soaking his Rooster's t-shirt.

"Are you camera shy?" I asked.

He didn't look up, still working fast and furious. He said, "You'll have to talk to him," pointing to the first clerk, not listening to a word I said and not seeming to care. And then he took off. I stood stuck and confused, again. Befuddled. I did what any reasonable person would do. I placed an order of ribs and waited.

Rich, the owner, looks more like a suburbanite than a guy who owns a BBQ rib place in the heart of inner city St. Paul. "I'm sorry, I was really busy," he said.

I explained, "I asked the first guy if I could interview him. He said to talk to you. You said to talk to him. It's pretty funny. Are you camera shy?"

"No, I'm not. Sure, you can interview me." Still sweating, his smile now brightened the room.

"Would you mind saying who you are, and give a shameless plug for your place?"

"Sure. I'm Rich, I'm the Rooster, the creator of all the barbeque around here, and we are some of the smokiest, tastiest, ribs in the country."

"How long have you been in business?"

"We opened our doors 24 years ago."

"I just got back from a barbeque tour. Also, I work at a correctional facility and the reason I'm here is because of a co-worker, Sweet Lou. He said this is the best place on the planet, bar none, so here I am."

Rich had a nice smile on his face. "There you go, man. Happy customers are the best advertising."

"It's hard to beat a good barbeque."

"A little word of mouth, yeah?" Rich said, still glowing. He emphasized his ribs are nice and smokey. "Do you like your ribs spicy?" he asked.

"No, I like the sweeter sauce."

Rich went to work. Smokey as advertised. And like all top-shelf barbeque places he doesn't leave his sides to chance. The French fries were golden and crisp; the coleslaw was chewy and full of the right amount of spicy flavor; the roll was fluffy and moist. I got a lot of ribs for a more than reasonable price. They don't list half-slab or full-slab on their menu. It just says RIBS.

Rich and Popeye's both kick out smokey ribs. The smokiness in Popeye's is subtle. Not true for Rich. His smokiness dominates front and center. It's the key feature of his ribs. The magic is that it isn't overpowering. It takes a master with the hands of a surgeon to be able to do that. The tenderness of the baby backs surprised me as the dirty brown color suggested rugged and rustic.

True to his word, he provided his own sauce, tilting it towards the sweet side.

A group of customers entered the building and they debated amongst themselves what to order. Overhearing their conversation, I interjected. I told Erick from Minneapolis, Wayne from Blaine, and Short Round from Chicago, "Go for the ribs," delivering a spiel on the trials and tribulations of the Mr. Y. BBQ Tour and Sweet Lou's ravings about Rooster's. "How did you guys end up at Rooster's on this day anyway?"

"A few weeks ago a buddy took me to Rooster's and I was hooked. We'd been golfing earlier today and dragged everyone here," Erick said.

"Other than Rooster's what do you think is the best rib place in the country?" I asked.

The answers came back Boney's in Denver, and Carson's in Chicago. But Wayne from Blaine, a novice in the fine art of barbeque, still rooted for Rooster's.

Their friend Jim joined later and he wasn't spared, I asked, "What place do you like best? Leave out Roo ...."

"ROOSTER'S!"

I answered my own question, "Leaving out Rooster's, I think Mark's Feed store in Louisville, Kentucky, is the best."

"What are some other good rib places in town?" Erick asked.

I said, "Big Daddy's is great. They are one of the best in the Twin Cities. I've also been to Rack Shack BBQ and Dickey's BBQ Pit, both in Burnsville. Dickey's is actually pretty good, nice and sweet. Kind of surprising. They were better than I thought they would be."

"I've been to Dickey's before," Erick said. "They're pretty good. There's another place I've been to near Uptown. I can't remember the name." Rudolph's?

The original clerk motioned me over, now wanting to be on camera. "When you asked me before I wasn't camera shy. I just didn't know what to say."

"Ok, cool. You're on now," *click*.

"Alright, Jeff from Rooster's." With that he waved goodbye.

* * *

There is something about theme-based trips that lures the soul and won't let go. It morphs into an irresistible addiction. In one case, a co-worker is a mere state away from realizing her lifelong dream of visiting all 50 state capitols. Only Louisiana stands in her way.

In another case a co-worker recently returned from the Four Corners area, where Arizona, Colorado, Utah, and New Mexico meet. He owns the moxy and praxis of common sense. He's a literal encyclopedia of something about something. Earlier in the summer he and his family motorcycled the banks of the Mississippi River exploring hole-in-the wall restaurants. Another idea he proffered, that others have done, is to travel to the highest point in all 50 states. Hearing about these trips charges me up.

Of course the theme-based Mr. Y. BBQ Tour worked its way into our conversation in a major way. Full of bubble, he cited an article entitled, *Best Barbeque*, in the July, 2010 issue of *Minnesota Monthly* magazine.

The author, Dara Moskowitz Grumdahl, had compiled a top ten list of the best BBQ places in Minnesota. I got pumped up and made contact with her via Facebook. She told me she had visited 40 different barbeque places throughout Minnesota. Her number one choice was Bob's Smoke Stack Ribs in Elgin, just outside Rochester.

Holding off as long as possible I scooted down on a bright, beautiful summer afternoon. Taking highway 52 seventy miles south of the Twin Cities, then east 15 miles placed me in tiny Elgin.

My search for Bob's Smoke Stack Ribs ended stuck at a T in the road. To the right, open farmland. In front, a strip mall. Making a left and then another left a short block later, downtown Elgin extended open arms. Parking the car and marching into the nearest door, I said, "Excuse me, I'm trying to find Bob's Smoke Stack Ribs. Do you know where they are?"

"Yes," the lady at the desk said. "Go back down the road in front to the first stop and make a right. It's a short ways further down on your left." Being the City Clerk, she would know.

Following her directions, Bob's was exactly where she had said it would be. I'm not quite sure how I missed them when my car had faced straight at them at the T. For some mysterious reason, the large black smoker sitting next to the huge **BOB'S SMOKE STACK RIBS** sign by the street wasn't enough. I hadn't had my eyes checked in a couple of years.

On the way into Bob's, in the parking lot with camera in hand, I started out, "Hi, this is Mr. Y. at Bob's Smokestack Ribs in tiny Elgin, Minnesota ...."

Small, homey, and clean, with Nascar memorabilia populating the walls, the tables were covered with red and white checkered table clothes, creating a picnic like neighborhood atmosphere.

Prices were more than reasonable. A mere $6 for a Quarter Rib Plate. Nice. The plate of ribs looked delicious. A zigzag drizzle of sauce coated them. Describing the sauce as super sweet is inaccurate. Sweet lite with no hint of tangy or spicy is better.

For sides, wedgy fries and baked beans. The beans were good, but not great. Most wedgy fries are made from an average size potato. They're easy to grab with one hand, plop in the mouth, and slosh down one after another, like peanuts. Most leave a bad potato paste aftertaste in the mouth, and a glass of water is needed to get them down the throat without choking.

Bob's wedgy fries told a far different story. It's possible they were made from football-size potatoes. It took almost two hands to hold one. Ok, a little exaggeration, but the point is that they weren't your neighbor's fries. They were cooked to a picture perfect golden brown with perfect texture, perfect crisp, and perfect crunch. They chewed into small, tasty, delightful morsels that slithered down the throat with teflon ease. They left no bad potato paste aftertaste and no glass of water needed. The positive mental images that I still have to this day are a testament to their grandeur nature.

Ms. Grumdahl, in her article, described Bob's ribs as custardy. Not thinking it the right word to use at the time, I now agree that would indeed be the right word to use. Custardy. They are tender, but not so tender that they fall off the bone. Dry, but not dry as when I say "my mouth is dry," and they weren't burned either.

They were smokey as in charcoal-type smokey, like when grilling hamburgers on a grill. Similar to Popeye's the smokiness sneaks up like the dark shadow of a spy rather than announcing itself like the opening bell on the New York Stock Exchange. Describing them presented more of a challenge for they contained some of the same qualities as other places, but in different variations of those qualities.

The bright sun, the blue sky, the perfect temperature, and no humidity made for a lazy afternoon. Relaxed and lethargic, I didn't have the desire to interview anyone. I existed in my own little world not wanting anyone or anything to disturb it.

Affixed high up in the corner above the door was a TV. The Rochester News Channel came on and as part of their newscast did an in-depth report on Bob's Smoke Stack Ribs. What? My inner competitor came to life.

I rocketed up to the counter with camera in hand. "I know you're not camera shy because I just saw you on TV," I said to Sue, white Caucasian, 5'3", short light brown hair, and wire-rimmed glasses. She giggled. I told her, "I love barbeque ribs and I just got back from a barbeque tour. Bob's Smoke Stack Ribs was listed as number one in the state of Minnesota in an article in the July, *Minnesota Monthly* magazine."

"We heard about that article," she answered.

Diedra, 5'6", an African-American, with short black hair, stood as a pair with Sue. "I was wondering what you were doing in the parking lot. I saw you out there with your camera."

"I was doing my little introduction."

"I thought you were part of the Biker Tour."

"No. Just little ole me. What's the Biker Tour? When you say biker do you mean biker as in riding a bicycle? Or do you mean biker as in motorcyclist?"

"A group came in that travels around the country on their motorcycles going from barbeque place to barbeque place to honor a fallen friend." A warm sense of camaraderie descended.

"How long has Bob's been in business?"

Sue chimed in, "We've been in Elgin for five years and Bob came from Arkansas."

Peering at Sue and Diedra, I asked, "Are these St. Louis-style ribs or Memphis-style ribs or Kansas City-style ribs," and now for the big punch line, "or are they Arkansas-style ribs?"

With puzzled looks at each other, they paused for a second or two before Diedra said, "They're Bob's ribs."

"Ohh."

Peering at them again, I went for the kill. "Can you tell me a little bit about Bob's secret for making great ribs?"

More puzzled looks, another long pause, and Diedra let loose "It's the love we put into them," bringing her words to a soft landing.

Mustering a whisper, I repeated, "Ohh, the love you put into them."

I had delivered the big punch line with my first question and went for the kill on the second. In both cases they bobbed and weaved, doing their version of the Rope-A-Dope, throwing answers back that left me meek, teetering, and perplexed. They're good. It's like they've done this before.

CHAPTER 9

boogalou territory

The beauty of my existence is I never know who I'm going to meet or when. On a breezy Minnesota evening, by happenstance, I met a woman from Louisville, Kentucky. I haven't failed to take note of the recurring Louisville theme that has come to my life.

I said to her, "I've been to Louisville before. I'm a huge Muhammad Ali fan. I went to the Ali Museum in downtown Louisville. It was great."

"In Kentucky basketball is king," she said. "We eat, sleep, and breathe basketball. We haven't forgotten him, we still love him, but basketball is king."

"Louisville is the Barbeque Capital of the world. I ate at Mark's Feed Store. It's the bomb!" I added, convinced this would impress her.

She didn't flinch, "Owensboro is the real Barbeque Capital. It's only 50 miles from Louisville. They have a big festival every year in May with bands and everything. 80,000 attend. You can't beat it. If you come on down, I'll be your tour guide."

This raised the bar on my curiosity, causing me to scramble for the nearest computer. It's true. Owensboro does declare itself *The Barbeque Capital of the World*. But wait, not so fast. I also did a Google search and three barbeque places showed up. In my way of thinking, there's no way they can be a Barbeque Capital if there are only three barbeque places. They're using a bait and switch to get tourists to visit. *Liars*. I hurled a stream of horribles at them.

But, I dug deeper:

from (owensboro.org)

Owensboro was first settled in 1797 and was originally known as "Yellowbanks" ... By 1817, the Act of Kentucky Legislature incorporated the town as "Owensborough."

from (boogaloubbq.com)

It all started in Owensboro, Kentucky. A Barbeque Mecca dating back to the late 1800's when Catholic churches started barbequing to raise money for their parishes, a tradition that continues to this day ... barbeque season starts with our BBQ Fest, which brings in as many as 80,000 in the second week of May ... each of the local Catholic churches holds its own barbeque each Saturday throughout the summer, ending with the Kentucky State BBQ Championship the last weekend of September.

The Owensboro-Daviess county Grillin and Chillin BBQ cook off was founded by Boogalou BBQ ... The cook off is a Kansas City Barbeque Society nationally sanctioned event that has more than $10,000 in prize money

-Roy Henry

A Barbeque Mecca with 80,000 barbeque-a-holics congregating every May? Strutting to music all day long? Catholic churches holding a BBQ fest every Saturday all summer long? A Grill'n and Chill'n BBQ cook off, nationally sanctioned, with a $10,000 prize? All this in tiny Owensboro? See you there, pal.

* * *

The surprises kept coming. Not long after Lisa Ocone left town to return to Indonesia, the phone rang. Then rang again. Then again, and again, and again. Worn out from the ceaseless ringing I picked up the phone. A voice on the other end said, "I'm hungry and I want to eat, let's go somewhere." It was The Fever, a long-time friend.

I suggested barbeque, and he was all for it, but he didn't like to leave the friendly confines of Richfield. Getting him to go anywhere meant moving mountains. He drove over and negotiations started.

"Let's go to Big Daddy's in St. Paul," I said.

"Nope, too far."

Exasperated, I said, "No it isn't, only takes ten maybe fifteen minutes to get there, and they have the best ribs in town."

"Nope, it has to be close," he responded, not budging.

"I'll drive."

"Nope," he said, being a stick in the mud.

After going round and round, we reached a compromise. Dickey's Barbeque Pit in Burnsville, the place Lisa Ocone and I had gone to a week earlier.

The Fever liked their barbeque, giving them a good rating. He ordered a pulled pork sandwich with a variety of sides, and loved their friendly customer service. He especially liked that he could purchase a Diet Coke for $2.50 and bring the large yellow cup back with him on other visits and get free refills. All the things Lisa Ocone liked about Dickey's, he liked too.

It didn't take much to please The Fever. There were two things in this world he loved more than anything else; Whoppers and Diet Coke. In The Fever's own words, "Suds and duds—never more than fifteen feet away."

CHAPTER 10

expecting it

Sitting in a big leather chair and watching TV late at night, the *ring, ring, ring* of the phone broke my nothingness. The name on the caller ID came as no surprise. I had been expecting it—Mr. McCoy. "Sir, I don't like how that guy in the video talked about Barbeque Sweets. I'm marinating a slab of ribs right now as we speak. I want you to come over Sunday and you can be the judge." The video of Tommy Campbell challenging him to a barbeque cage match ate him alive. He couldn't stay silent.

A few weeks later on my way to work at summer school at the juvenile correctional facility in Minnetonka, Minnesota, the urge for a donut at Yo-Yo Donut and Coffee Bar proved overwhelming; I salivated over the prospects of a mango green ice tea and a white frosted mini-bismarck with blueberry filling.

Honk, honk, honk. Who's honking at me, I wondered. *Honk, honk, honk.* Scanning the parking lot, I saw him. Mr. McCoy, flashing that broad smile. Excited, it wasn't too hard to convince him to come into Yo-Yo. The bribe of a glazed donut and Coke goes a long way in building friendships.

As a star basketball player in high school, and now a fiery basketball coach, he couldn't shake his competitive fire. Standing in line, in a sleepy tone, he said, "Sir, tell that guy in the video Barbeque Sweets has just been declared the Champion of the Aurora Block BBQ Cook Off in St. Paul, Minnesota. I won with a whole pork shoulder. You tell him that, sir."

"I will," I said.

A few weeks later, out of the blue, he sent me a text message:

McCoy Family Reunion, August 20th

On that bright Sunday afternoon he walked me over to an oversize platter in the middle of a food stuffed table. "These are my mom's ribs, sir. You try them."
"Are yours the same as hers?"
"They're similar. Load up."
I did as ordered. In fact, I loaded so much onto my plate I had to spend an inordinate amount of time balancing the food on the pile just right so the whole thing wouldn't tip over. In the end it took both hands to carry it. How could I carry more, I thought, upon seeing his relatives lay out another spread on a dubious table number two. On the fly I devised a brilliant game plan.

First, focus on and devour plate number one, leaving it spick and span clean. Second, walk fast—no run—back to table two. Three, load up plate number two, spending large amounts of time on the delicate balancing act so that pile wouldn't tip over. Four, slide over to table one and scoop up a few more of mom's ribs. Five, glide outside and find a pleasant location in which to gorge. Six, gorge.

Step one went down without a hitch, speedy and greedy. Steps two, three, and four occurred with the efficiency only found among Navy Seals. Seamless. At this point the burning desire to bite into mom's ribs turned into desperate restraint. Step five, finding the perfect location at a picnic table underneath a colorful blooming tree ... easy, like beating Sandifer in Ping Pong. Step six presented the biggest challenge.

The problem had to do with portion control. It didn't exist. No human could eat at such a sustained pace. Reality stepped in, and my consumption rate slowed to a near halt as the pile on the plate shrank closer and closer to sea level.

I ate so much my stomach hurt badly and I literally wanted to vomit. Barbeque Sweets had a camera in his hand and wanted me to snap pictures of him and his family. I obliged. He's got such a cool family. But the whole time I was seconds away from letting it fly—he never knew the truth.

I observed him bounce from table to table beaming a broad smile, knowing mom's ribs had made their mark. Later, he bounced from grill-to-grill doling out expert tips that only he could give. Not far away, on his own grill, chicken wings coated with his secret sauce waited in patient solitude to be devoured. Smiling, portion control wasn't in his vocabulary either.

CHAPTER 11

fall is the best time of year

Fall is my favorite time of year. It isn't hot and muggy like during the summer, and doesn't offer the bitter cold of winter. The leaves have changed to a collage of rustic colors, and the air has a certain crispness to it. A new school year had just begun bringing with it unforeseen triumphs and tragedies. But despite all this, the search for the perfect barbeque must carry on.

On one particularly colorful evening Pete and Greg left a voicemail message. They were going up to Q-Fanatic BBQ in Champlain, Minnesota, a suburb of Minneapolis. I had told them about Ms. Grumdahl's article and how she rated Q-Fanatic as number two in the state. For weeks Pete had wanted to meet up there as it was a stone's throw away from a class he taught in Coon Rapids.

Answering the cell phone is not a strength of mine. Don't even ask about voicemail. I hate them both. It cost me. They came back flying high, outright pumped, like madmen after an out-of-body experience. They rated Q-Fanatic as high as Ms. Grumdahl did. Memories of blown opportunities, like Chicago, came to pass. It plain hurt. But all was not lost as the autumn offered other unexpected opportunities.

Mr. Carter, a humble giant, originates from the heart of BBQ country, Memphis, Tennessee. At 6 ft 7 inches tall he played college basketball for the University of Minnesota, reaching number seven on the Gopher's all-time rebounder list with 736 rebounds. Later he played professionally in Europe.

Tapping his brain before I left on the Mr. Y. BBQ Tour, I asked, "What's the best place, anywhere, for barbeque?"

"Do you mean like a regular restaurant or any place?"

"Any place."

"Interstate in Memphis. It's a hole in the wall, but there's no place like it."

When school resumed in the fall word spread about my tour. Not shocking, since it was announced at our all-staff meeting. My newfound celebrity status gained traction. Co-workers approached, like autograph seekers, in the deep recesses of the hallways to tell me of their favorite barbeque places.

Mr. Carter, upon seeing me in the main hallway during workshop week asked, "Have you ever heard of a place called Baldy's in Lakeville?"

"No."

"I've been hearing about them, they are supposed to be really good."

"Man, now I want to go down there and check them out."

Casting a long shadow, he flashed a big smile. "I want to go check them out, too."

"We should both agree to check them out so that we can compare notes," I said.

"Agreed," he replied.

Two days later, karma struck. "Have you heard of a place called Baldy's? All the truckers say it is really good, one of their favorites. It's in Lakeville, off exit 81. Again, it's called Baldy's or something like that," the voice mail from Tami the Trucker said.

Thoughts of Baldy's ping-ponged around my brain for a few days before I made the decision to bolt down there. Just off 35W, they were easy to find. Housed in a large structure inside a mini strip mall, they had a colorful sports bar theme with TVs strategically placed throughout for optimum viewing.

Their ribs had a pink hue to them, like when meat is more raw than cooked. By themselves the ribs were bland and pasty. But a magical, scientific transformation took place when sauces were added.

There are four different ones—Spicy, Gold, Original, and Sweet. Gold and Sweet were the runaway front runners with Sweet being the Champ. The name speaks for itself. Gold was less sweet, a tiny bit tangy, but an original flavor. Like Arthur Bryant's, it was the combination of rib and sauce that made it an experience.

The traditional side fare of beans and fries were nothing special. Out of a burning need to spruce up the fries I sloshed the sauces on them without reserve. This proved to be a brilliant stroke, changing them into worthy contenders.

Fresh off the Baldy's experience, an unforeseen happening occurred amongst the co-workers at school. Their egos returned. No longer did they swarm to tell of their favorite barbeque places, they came to change the narrative. They gloated and strutted with a swagger I hadn't seen before. As masters in the art of bragging, they spared no expense, elevating their ribs to new highs while sending others to new lows.

Who's the best? Ribfest! The only rational way to settle the score meant organizing a show down. Put up or shut up, mano-e-mano. Recruiting wasn't hard. Ribfest contestants lined up, stoked by their egos.

Recruitment efforts included Rod, one of the school chefs. Finding him slaving away in the school kitchen, I started in: "This summer I went on a barbeque tour in search for the perfect barbeque and everyone here brags about how great their ribs are. It's time to settle the question. I'm organizing a Ribfest to find out who's the best. Do you want to enter? This is a chance to show what you got."

"Sounds interezing, but no thanks, I am too busy, but check deez out," he said, his Serbian accent clear and precise. He took out a card from his wallet and handed it to me. It read *Certified Barbeque Judge (CBI), Kansas City Barbeque Society* (out of date by two months from lack of renewal).

"Not only that, but I have been on five, count'm five, barbeque tours."

"Really? Where did you go?"

"I been to the east, south and southeast, all da big barbeque areas. I got pictures of everything."

"How many BBQ cookoffs have you judged?"

"I've judged 300 to 400 contests."

"Do you ever get sick of barbeque?"

"No. Never. If you ever want to know where to go, you talk to me first. I will tell you and I have tons of pictures. I will show dem to you sometime."

"WOW! Also, I met this woman from Louisville who told me Owensboro, Kentucky, is the Barbeque Capital of the World. Have you ever been there?"

Staring at me for a few seconds, he seemed to be processing. He said, "They all say dat. There is a place in North Carolina that says they are da Barbeque Capital of the World and they have a population of 10,000. They only had 11 barbeque places. They all say dat."

"What training is required to become a Certified Barbeque Judge?"

He went on to explain that a trainer from the Kansas City Barbeque Society gives training sessions a couple of times a year in different areas of the country. In Rod's case it was an all-day Saturday seminar at a hotel in a suburb north of Minneapolis. The trainer is not only a judge, but enters contests too. The trainer made ribs at the seminar and they all sat around and enjoyed them.

"Nah doo difficult," Rod concluded.

At Ribfest we had five different types of ribs made by five different contestants. We had sides to last a month. Beans, coleslaw, corn bread muffins, potato salad, and corn on the cob with plenty of pop to drink. Our special needs interpreter delivered blow-by-blow commentary on my blog at mrybarbeque.trumblr.com.

When I made the official announcement over the intercom, "Ribfest is on," the masses swarmed around the corner at breakneck speed. It's as though they had been camped there a long time waiting for the announcement, like shoppers on Black Friday. In the blink of an eye ribs disappeared, like your bank balance after the bank takes their fees.

In the normal course of a day serious faces take care of serious business. Conversations get intense as staff works to defuse tough situations. Now, a transformation took place. Electricity flowed from every corner. Happy faces abounded, and cheery conversations filled the tables. Seriousness couldn't be found and tensions disappeared.

We were short of ribs, but how? Someone (*not me, not me*) forgot to bring out the other platter of ribs for contestant number two. Bringing out the missing platter, an announcement was made and the ribs on it disappeared in nanoseconds.

Our unscientific vote as to who was the best got complicated. Mr. Carter made pulled pork southern style, meaning he put coleslaw on top of the meat in each sandwich. For selfish reasons I asked him to bring one extra slab of ribs. Instead he brought two.

Mr. McCoy became a last-minute addition ending up with three slabs. Each of the other contestants brought five slabs each. One brought a total of six slabs, five for the competition and a secret non-voting slab in the kitchen. So you see, our voting had no choice but to be unscientific.

By the time I got to eating, all the ribs were gone.

Using time-tested scavenger skills, I scrapped a few bones from the second platter for contestant two. Added to that was a nib of meat hidden in the tin foil from contestant four. A raid on the secret slab in the kitchen scored more booty. Mr. Carter reached over the masses and placed the last bone from his slab directly into my hands. Beautiful.

After the unscientific votes had been tallied, Mr. Carter took home the championship. His ribs were something special. Not that the others weren't, but his had a different mojo. Taking a singular bite into the rib, the raw smokey barbeque flavor burst onto the scene. After a slight time delay, it hit ... a combination of slight fruity orange and an oh so slight tangy bite. Putting it all together his ribs had an original, authentic, down-home Tennessee barbeque flavor that satisfied the most scrutinizing palate. Barbequey, smokey, sweet, orangey, slightly tangy, all combined into one.

The history teacher, Mr. Lampert, had the right idea though. "Declare it a draw. A draw! Our table couldn't decide. They were all so great! Declare it a draw!"

For the record, Mr. McCoy tied for second in the unscientific voting. Telling him later that his ribs disappeared like lightning made him walk with an extra bounce, smiling broader and longer than at any other time in the fall.

I said to him, "Sir, I've got something to tell you. I've tasted your mom's ribs, but I still haven't tasted yours. By the time I got to eating, your ribs were gone."

Mr. McCoy, with that puppy dog look, paused for a moment, and said slow and direct, "Don't worry, sir. I'm going to cook up a slab and bring it in just for you and me." In our Ribfest video he uncorked a challenged back to Tommy Campbell. "Tell him I said to come on up to St. Paul, Minnesota."

CHAPTER 12

i didn't plan for this

Poor planning, winging it, and laziness robbed me the last time. But not this time. I'm a man of my word. What's all the fuss? Well, I'm getting ready for a trip to Chicago to eat BBQ ribs at I-57. A desire to be soulful and altruistic with the singular purpose of going to I-57 is, in reality, a bold and untruthful lie. There is another more pressing matter. With great sadness it must be reported that my longtime friend, The Fever, died when struck by a car. This happened a week after we went to Dickey's BBQ Pit. Life throws us curveballs and this certainly was one of them.

I won't lie. This was a serious blow. I didn't receive the news as though merely catching a speeding baseball. Rather, it struck deep in my heart causing an outright detour. It hurt—bad.

Knowing him for over 30 years he was family to us, an energetic soul who could lift your spirits in the darkest hour. Defined by humor and believing in persistence, with regular routine he drove all of us nuts with nonstop phone calls. I am not understating this. After he got us to the point of strangling him, in the next breath, he would have us Rolling On the Floor Laughing (ROFL).

He bellowed *beautiful, baby, beautiful!* with bombastic frequency, and his flag pants became a characteristic signature. Other times, donning his green Edina hockey jersey and tie-dyed colored wig, he breathed *unhunkered and on fire!* The most important thing you need to know about The Fever? With great enthusiasm he was an editor of the very book you are reading.

My impending trip to Chicago is first and foremost because of The Fever, and second, to eat ribs. A little background will help you understand why.

In the early 1990s he and I traveled to Chicago by Amtrak train to see a Minnesota North Star vs. Chicago Blackhawks NHL hockey game at old Chicago Stadium in west Chicago. His dad knew Walter Bush, the founder of the North Stars, and secured three tickets for us five rows behind the goalie.

The Fever had been warned to skip the idea that he could work late into the night and leave for Chicago early the next morning. The sleep deprivation would be too much.

"Oh no, I'll be fine, not a problem," he said.

Cranky as an old coot all the way to Chicago, he complained about this, that, and everything in between. At breakfast the next morning in downtown, he complained, pouted, and whined about his entire existence, scrunching his face and spitting tacks about everything under the sun.

Glaring at him and mad as a hornet's nest, I said, "I didn't come to Chicago after 15 years just to listen to you whine and complain and carry on like a little baby. I told you not to leave the next morning after getting no sleep the night before. That's your fault, not mine. I'm giving you two choices. You can either shape up and we can continue on or you can keep whining and enjoy Chicago by yourself because you won't be hanging around me. I'm perfectly fine continuing on by myself, and I'll get home just fine without having to listen to you pout about everything. Which is it?"

He didn't see that coming. Score one for the Timster. His downward scrunching angry eyebrows shot straight up in bewilderment. His clenched jaw and gritted teeth opened wide, like when a dentist says *open wide please*. You could cut the air with a knife.

After a long deafening pause he got up and left, storming across the street. I watched him. Head down, shoulders slumped. Brood, stomp, stomp, stomp. Turn around. Brood, stomp, stomp, stomp. Turn around. Brood, stomp, stomp, stomp. Turn around. For minutes on end I witnessed this cycle of brood, stomp, and turn when he eventually returned back to the seat in front of me.

Watching The Fever beg for forgiveness is satisfying and ROFL. His voice changed to *baaaaby* talk. He begged like a remorseful toddler exhibiting no shame. By the time he finished his retribution, he had me in stitches. He said, "I am proud of you for doing that to me, you stood up for yourself. You should do that more often. Don't let people push you around. You put me in my place and I respect you more for that."

I let him have it. "You kept whining over and over and wouldn't quit. I couldn't take it anymore. I warned you about coming on this trip straight from work with no sleep. Someone had to put you in your place. Ok, fine, you're back in the inner circle." Being back in the inner circle made our trip whole again. I made him leave the tip. A big one, too.

We did all the things tourists do in Chicago. We attended the Blackhawks game, visited the Shedd Aquarium, toured the Natural History Museum, and walked through the University of Chicago. We even witnessed a man go nuts on a subway platform late at night in the heart of South Chicago.

We toured up and down Michigan Avenue and explored all we could, ending up at the John Hancock Center, 102 stories tall, at 9:30 pm at night. After reading in the lobby about the history of the building, we boarded the elevator for a fast ride to the top ready to enter the observation deck.

Going first I paid the $3.63 entry fee and walked through the turnstiles. The Fever stayed behind and stood motionless by a window, his back to the turnstiles.

"What are you doing?"

"I'm not coming in."

"Why not? Is it the money? I'll pay the $3.63."

He stood there arms crossed, "Nope, I 'm not coming in."

In stunned silence, I said, "I don't get it. Are you afraid of heights?"

"Nope. I'm just not coming in," arms still crossed.

Conceding defeat and frustrated, I continued in alone. The breathtaking nighttime view proved to be a once-in-a-lifetime experience, colorful and serene in the same sentence. But it wasn't as much fun without The Fever.

The following year I called from the top of the Hancock Center and rubbed it in. I said to The Fever, "Can you guess where I am? Ha ha ha ha. I'm at the top of the John Hancock Center, someplace you'll never see in your lifetime."

Through the phone line came back a boisterous, "HA HA HA HA HA, I'm never going to the top of the Hancock Center!"

"You owe me a trip to the top of the Hancock Center."

"No I don't."

When a famous celebrity passed away The Fever would put the back of his hand to his mouth and say in a whispering voice, "He's not gonna make it to the Hancock Center," adding a *pppsssssssst* and a giggle.

Never missing an opportunity to pounce, I called him up another time, "Hey, do you want to do something tonight?"

"Nope."

"Why not?"

"Don't want to."

Mustering the best WWE announcer voice I could, I bellowed, "THE FEVER HATES LEAVING THE FRIENDLY COOONFINES OF RICHFIELD!"

"HA HA HA HA," came back the reply through the phone line.

"Come on Fever, get out of your little cell. Let's go do something, a movie, something."

"Nope."

I lowered my voice over the phone to a low hushed tone, like whispering a secret. I said, "The Fever's not gonna make it to the top of the Hancock Center."

He mimicked, if not mocked me, back. That was part of his cat and mouse game. In a low hushed tone, like whispering his own secret, he said, "The Fever's not going to make it to the top of the Hancock Center."

"You owe me a trip to the top of the John Hancock Center."

"No I don't," he repeated, giving credence to Newton's Third Law: for each action there is an equal and opposite reaction.

"Yes you do. You're not getting off this easy."

"No, I'm not."

"Bye."

"Ok, bye." *Click.*

Over the years The Fever gave the illusion of being hooked. Perks were his Achilles heel. A well-timed offer of suds and duds, and he would be like putty in my hands. Once, I put an offer on the table to do all the driving and pay his share of the tolls if he would take the two days to go to Chicago and make good on his debt. He made a believer out of me, but in the end, he never did make it. I sank in dejection; it pleased him, to know he defeated me.

Cat fights were frequent. "Why won't you go to the top of the Hancock Center? What's the big deal? You owe me a trip to the top of the Hancock Center," I said once, a little steamed.

"I went to Chicago with my dad 30 years ago, that counts."

"That doesn't count. You have to go with me to count." I was ready to beat him over the head with a hammer.

"Yeah, it does count, and I don't care," he said in delight.

"Fever, when you die, I am going to put on your tombstone, 'Here lies The Fever. He never made it to the Hancock Center.'"

"HA HA HA HA HA!" He bellowed out of the phone, "Here lies The Fever, he never made it to the Hancock Center. HA HA HA HA HA!"

At one point he clued me in on his true dream: to attend an event, anything, at Wembley Stadium in London, England. As a kid his family traveled there and those memories stuck with him.

"I'll go with you to Wembley Stadium if you go to the top of the Hancock Center," I said.

"Forget it. I'm not doing it."

"Come on Fever you have to fly in and out of Chicago to get to London anyways."

"No, I won't do it and I don't care. I want to go to Wembley Stadium. I saw Chicago with my dad years ago, close enough."

I shifted into WWE announcer mode again, "HERE LIES THE FEVER. HE NEVER MADE IT TO THE HANCOCK CENTER!"

"HA HA HA HA! Here lies The Fever, he never made it to the Hancock Center," he bellowed back.

This past summer I *knew* I had him hooked. "Fever, you owe me a trip to the Hancock Center. You're not getting off this easy."

"I'll do it. I will. I'll do it. Just tell me when."

"What?" I did a double take immersed in doubt.

"I said I'll go."

"Fever, will you ever tell me why you didn't go

through the turnstiles? Why did you stand in the hall-way?"

He thought for a moment and gave the only honest answer he would ever give. "Well, I don't really know, I was really tired and exhausted and I am not really sure. I just didn't feel like it."

My soul reached out and believed him. Hope sprang eternal, confidence abounded. But despite the apparent honesty and goodwill, he struck like a thief in the night, still never leaving the friendly confines of Richfield.

During the last year I nailed him good. I repeated to him on occasions too numerous to count my familiar phrase, "When you die, I am going to write on your tombstone, 'Here lies The Fever. He never made it to the Hancock Center.'" Unfortunately, this never seemed to faze him.

The Fever beamed with pride one night when pulling out a worn tattered scrapbook. Pasted into it was an old yellowed newspaper article about a Coe College football game written by a gritty sportswriter named David Richmond Pearson, A.K.A. The Fever. Bright sparks of energy lit up the room as he recounted the glory days of years past when he cruised from campus-to-campus snaring scoops.

I became tantalized by this and saw the possibilities. I reached into my pocketbook and recruited him to be an editor for this book. I couldn't offer him riches, but I did offer him a few bucks. Soon, an agreement was reached. David Richmond Pearson, A.K.A. The Fever, became my Senior-Editor-in-Chief.

Being an editor, then and now, brought him to life. After handing him a fresh copy of the manuscript he would stay up late at night editing, punching away on that old manual beat-up typewriter of his.

He kept pestering me, "When are you going to give me more editing for your book? I'm ready. Come on, give me more."

"Fever, I need to first incorporate your current edits before I have more for you. Give me a chance to incorporate these edits first. There will be more editing, just not right now."

"When are you going to give me more to edit? I'm ready. Come on. Give me more. I'm ready."

* * *

On that early September Sunday afternoon, only two months after getting back from the tour, my dad told me to get out to the kitchen, "*Now!*" Not having a clue why, I figured it had something to do with taking out the garbage or raking leaves. But then Ethan's voice, a friend of The Fever's, echoed through the hallways. I knew something was wrong. Ethan said something about the police, knocking on the door, and the caretaker.

Knowing how to react remained elusive. My emotions weren't prepared. The night before The Fever had gone across the street from his apartment to get suds and duds. Coming back he was struck by a car, by accident. He passed away on the spot. Just a day earlier he'd been over mowing our yard. Something he loved to do with regular routine; I am not understating this.

The last few years had been rough for him. He once ignored our pleas to pay a traffic ticket and ended up cuffed and in jail, unceremoniously dumped. Describing his difficulties he liked to state, "Fired five times, fore-closed twice, arrested twice, jailed *once*."

But mention the word edit and the kid in the candy store came roaring to the scene, like a politician at a photo op. Pumped up, he gave a plug to the class he was taking at Normandale Community College about my book. He put up flyers advertising his editing services. He was, and I quote, "*Unhunkered and on fire!*"

Talking to him by phone on that fateful day he was pissed. No one had called him about helping Pete move. My great fun was rubbing it in; knowing it would get a rise. By the end of the conversation he was back to his old self.

"Let's go see a movie. How about tonight? Come on, let's go," he said.

"Sure Fever, sure," I answered, lacking enthusiasm.

"How about some more editing on the book? Come on. I'm ready. Give me more. I'm ready. When are you going to give me more? I'm ready, come on. Do it!"

Hustling off the phone to avoid his pestering, I had other plans—a trip down the road to Baldy's BBQ, not knowing what lay ahead. I've been asked before, "Why are you always in such a hurry?" I still don't have a good answer.

Our family went through the grieving process like anyone would do for a family member. Tears flowed. We made the coolest YouTube video ever honoring him, bringing a small amount of healing and closure.

His family chose cremation, and at his memorial service the packed sanctuary was in somber silence. His niece broke down during a reading. Not a dry eye in the house, a Kleenex tissue in every hand.

Mimicking The Fever's flair for the dramatic, his Pastor told the story of The Fever coming up after a service once and saying, *You know, there's a lot of sinners out there*!! stealing a line from Clint Eastwood, and finishing with, *We gotta fill these seats!*

"The Fever probably said that line to me a 100 times" the Pastor said. We at the service who had gathered to mourn now burst into laughter. The tears of sadness turned to tears of joy. Only The Fever, only The Fever. Even in death he delivered his unique brand of humor.

After negotiating with the family they agreed to give us some of his ashes. I know, I know. Somber and sinister. Take heart. There's a method to the madness. You'll see. Now sits The Fever in a little metal container in our China cabinet. The Fever is still with us, persistent and refusing to go.

I told myself I was going to march over to The Fever's tombstone and plop a post-it note on it:

Here lies The Fever. He NEVER made it to the top of the Hancock Center.

I warned him. It wasn't an idle threat. One day a bolt of inspiration overcame me. A new idea emerged, a much better one. Why not take The Fever, in his little metal container, to the top of the John Hancock Center in Chicago? He would have to go because he wouldn't have a choice. He owed me a trip to the top and I wasn't too keen on letting him off the hook. Maybe it wouldn't be the way he planned it, but he would be going, flag pants and all. And he wouldn't be charged admission.

My new dream? To slap this post-it note on his tombstone:

Here lies The Fever. He FINALLY made it to the top of the Hancock Center.

The dream is coming true. The Fever would be proud, the fact that he is getting all this attention. Up in the Great Eternal he is giving high fives at a fever pitch. *Beautiful Baby, Beautiful!*

Thanks to The Fever, I-57 BBQ here I come. Don't worry Fever. There will be much editing to do and I'll be looking to you for inspiration. After all, you are my Senior-Editor-in-Chief. See you in Heaven, my friend.

CHAPTER 13

paid in full

The three of us hopped in the car around 1 pm. Anytime we are together in a confined space there is reason for concern. Issues rise, tempers flare, conflicts happen, and getting along becomes a struggle.

We each had high hopes for this trip on Thanksgiving Day when we skipped the idea of staying home and cooking a traditional turkey, choosing to drive to Chicago instead.

We took I-94 east out of Minneapolis, cut through straight barren brown land, followed by stretches of barren brown rolling hills, followed by more stretches of straight barren brown land, followed by even more stretches of barren brown rolling hills ... you get the idea.

Stopping at Ho-Chunk casino in central Wisconsin we munched on a Thanksgiving buffet. It was good, but not great. We sampled a little bit of everything, including turkey, ham, and BBQ ribs that earned an unassuming OK. Mass buffets, in general, focus on bulk rather than quality. I gave this one a passing grade in order to keep the holiday spirit alive and in the moment, rather than casting a mean, dark pall.

Nearing Madison, Wisconsin, Pete needed convincing to continue along I-94. He struggles making simple decisions, going in emotional circles for a while, and eventually comes back to no decision. I have learned to be precise and forceful.

"Take I-94 to Milwaukee."

"Are you sure? Isn't it quicker to take I-90?"

"No. Take I-94."

"Are you sure?"

"Yes."

We arrived at the Wyndham Garden Hotel in Buffalo Grove, Illinois, at 10:30 pm, taking The Fever in his little metal container up to our room for the night.

No one wanted to share a bed. My siblings brought inflatable air mattresses. The mattresses inflate by way of an electric pump, taking three minutes each to inflate. They were more like inflatable rafts than anything. I offered to bring along my ever reliable sleeping pad, but that got mocked.

We always have great plans where we are all going to do everything together as one big happy family. But in reality it never turns out that way. The next morning, at the buffet, optimism reined when we discussed our agenda items. Crossing off each item would take three months to accomplish; we had three days.

On this trip, chowing down on BBQ at I-57 took second place. The Fever and the Hancock Center dominated all else. Parking in nearby Arlington Heights, we planned to take the train into downtown Chicago with The Fever packed safe and secure in my backpack.

The neighborhood had a splattered density containing a desirable variety of shops and living spaces. Newer and more modern, yet old world with a distinct European feel, everything from the large chateau-like buildings to the angular shaped hut of the train station itself.

"This is how it looked in Perth when I went to Australia," I said.

I heard exuberant exhortations of, "Wow. This really seems like Europe!"

"This is how it looked in Perth when I went to Australia," I repeated.

I heard more exuberant exhortations of, "Wow. This really seems like Europe!"

Giving in to his insatiable habit, Greg went outside

the station to smoke, on the opposite side of the building, away from the tracks. "Where's Greg?" I soon asked.

"He's out smoking" Pete said.

"I am not chasing after him. It's up to him to be aware of when the train comes. If he misses it, he has a cell phone and he can meet us in downtown Chicago." I set a firm unwavering boundary.

"Well, ah, well ...."

The train light, though visible in the distance, never seemed to get closer, remaining a small dot pinching the daylight. An explanation soon came pouring out of the loudspeaker. The train would be delayed by 10-15 minutes, "due to heavy Black Friday passenger traffic." But soon the explanation changed to, "a customer dispute."

At that precise moment in time Mother Nature called, and the train delay provided an opportunity to take care of business. Sitting on a hard cold seat in the bathroom stall—without warning—the earth underneath shook and rumbled. The shaking and rumbling left me quite nervous, so I did my best to speed up nature's process and hustled out to the tracks with cell phone in hand, only to discover the train being boarded. I was only a few miserable seconds away from becoming a victim of my own sermonizing. *Arrghhh.*

The double-decker train car rose in the air like a London double-decker bus. Regular rows of seats decorated the bottom deck while the top deck demanded more attention due to its unique seat arrangement.

Two long rows of seats were on each side of the rail car, separated by a huge open space from floor to ceiling, allowing for the ultimate in people watching below. Also, every half dozen rows the seats changed from facing forward to facing inward. The cramped arrangement made for difficult walking, similar to the upper walkways of a prison cell block, like in the movies.

The train ride soon transformed the reasonable passenger into a state of calm and tranquility, allowing for a series of *aha* moments as the world moved by in slow windy motion. For some strange reason, I find sitting in a dentist's chair has the same effect.

Greg and I each obtained a $5 scratch-off ticket, and good fortune fell on me as I won $100. Looking for cheap entertainment, we made sure to call Pete and rub it in.

The conductor, ah, the conductor. He possessed a gruff veteran demeanor which struck me as keenly accurate to the stereotype of a conductor. He brandished a striking resemblance to Brendan Gleeson, the Irish actor known for portraying thugs and bad guys. The conductor's 6' 3" frame cast a long shadow, and his chiseled face loomed over seated passengers. He wore a navy blue uniform and his short reddish hair stuck straight out from underneath the short, but round and boxy conductor cap.

He looked to be in his mid-50s as evidenced by a moderate size belly hanging over the belt, hiding the change maker attached to it. Every now and then I would hear the *clink, clink* of coins when he made a ticket sale.

Greg, ever the Vikings fan, chanted at him, "Go Vikings, go Vikings, go Vikings."

Standing stiff and stoic, icy in his glare, the conductor said, "Don't even go there." It was hard not to notice the rough and gruff edge to his voice.

I started chanting, "Go Bears, go Bears, go Bears," in an attempt to alter his mood. It worked. Our good friend the conductor now changed to glowing smiles and a happier persona.

Greg and I searched frantically for a seat in the passenger-stuffed first car. "Should we sit here?" we asked the conductor with the utmost in humility.

"FOLLOW ME!" he blasted in a deep baritone voice bouncing with authority. The sound waves from his words resonated into a sonic boom upon our collective eardrums. Stunned by the shock and awe, we stood timid. Defeated, we shuffled after him to the next car like prisoners of war.

Now on the train's public address system, the conductor spoke slowly in his deep baritone, scolding every humble passenger, "Listen, and listen carefully. Do not, I repeat, do not board the train for your return trip without having first purchased a ticket at the station." His spoke in verifiable slow motion. "Do not, I repeat, do not, board the train for your return trip without first purchasing a ticket at the station. The main station is always open, the outlying areas are not." His monotone lecture made me reminisce over stern lectures of years past from dear old dad, scolding me for something I hadn't done yet.

After leaving the station, some of us $100 richer, confusion reigned as to how to get to Navy Pier. An apparent homeless man, seizing the opportunity, wasted no time in evoking his hustle. Such hustle, built into the DNA of every citizen of Chicago at birth, is an instinctive reflexive reaction triggered by the scent of money. There are no exceptions.

"I hope you can give me a little cash, being it's Thanksgiving. I know you will and I know you are gonna take care of me good." The art of persuasion is a natural gift to those blessed with his particular DNA.

"This is your lucky day," I answered, "for I am feeling generous, and I am going to take care of you." With infinite wisdom I handed over a $20 bill from the small stack of bills jammed in my wallet.

"Thanks, man," he said, grabbing the $20, and scooting off to his next hustle job.

"How much did you give him?" my siblings asked.

"$20."

"What?" They gasped.

"It's Thanksgiving. I was feeling generous."

"Oh," they said in unison, gasping one final time.

At Navy Pier, with the John Hancock Center as a backdrop, bystanders posed for pictures with The Fever, ignorant of our goal at hand. The Fever didn't like this forced march towards the goal, but he trudged along like the trooper he didn't want to be.

My need for urban biking is an obsession. Nothing frustrated this obsession more than finding the CLOSED FOR THE SEASON sign hanging on the door of the bike rental shop on the Pier. An attempt to find another rental shop on the East River Docks led to walking in circles, which ignited a short stroll into a long hike. Bike shops in Chicago exhibit a common behavior of posting hours on their door, but not following them.

While I dreamed of biking, Greg drooled over the prospects of purchasing a Bear's hat at Soldier Field, and Pete wanted to hang out everywhere.

To achieve these goals we would use the water ferry, where I would depart at Michigan Avenue, and they would get off at the Sears Tower—a curious game plan at best. The goal was to meet at Millennium Park, right next to Michigan Avenue. Yet they bought $7 tickets to the Sears Tower, with no real interest in visiting the Sears Tower, and not real close to Michigan Avenue either. My ticket only cost $4.

* * *

Infinite shoppers, bustling up and down Michigan Avenue in search of the ultimate bargain, belayed an energy that in physics terms would be defined as Brownian Motion. My superior multitasking skills proved to be an asset, for I participated in the nonstop density of the human race while in a selfish search for the ultimate in people watching. For this I achieved victory.

Thronged cheers and grateful claps rose above the street like shockwaves. Drawn to the beehive of activity, I rushed across the street, heading kitty corner from Millennium Park. Hearing the voices of the performers thundering up into the atmosphere, I headed into a trot.

As a group of twentysomthing African-American street performers, they were remarkable in their ability to work a crowd. In fact, a Communications Professor I know would give them an A+ for entertainment value and ingenious creativity. They sang, told jokes, jumped, flipped, and ripped on the audience, all in good fun, not leaving out a poke or two at the stereotype of inner city black men. "You can pay us now or pay us later when we take the TV at your house later tonight. Not laughing now are you?"

Scared souls knelt in a row on the sidewalk as the star performer ran full tilt and flipped over their entirety, landing safely on his feet on the far side of them, like Evil Kneivel jumping cars.

I pulled The Fever out of my backpack so he could get a close up view. I'm sure I heard him hooting and hollering, slapping high fives with everyone. It's debatable whether the performer who held The Fever actually understood he held a dead man's ashes. I'm sure I heard an unmistakable din emerge from that little metal container: "Boy, do they look good!"

I eventually strolled back across the street to Millennium Park, and striking rental gold, I found perhaps the lone open bike shop in all of Chicago. When confronted with a choice between a female-style bike or no bike at all I came to the conclusion that beggars can't be choosey.

With me at every push of the bike pedal was The Fever resting comfortably in the deep recesses of my back pack. I took him out to enjoy each and every activity encountered on our journey from Millennium Park to the Hershey's Store.

First, The Fever participated in an Occupy Wall Street Protest marching down the sidewalk. There he was heard to say, "Bitter, bitter."

At the Water Tower we had a religious experience

while listening to a group of determined Spiritual Prophets who exhorted the masses, "EITHER REPENT OF YOUR SINS AND LIVE OR BURN IN HELL FOREVER!"

The Fever exhorted the masses himself, delivering his own version of a religious experience: "YOU KNOW, THERE'S A LOT OF SINNERS OUT THERE!" The Spiritual Prophets had no answer for that.

I would be remiss if I didn't note the packed sidewalks with Black Friday shoppers the likes of which I've never seen. Normally one can ride on Michigan Avenue and with relative ease navigate the tiny amount of space between traffic and sidewalk. When that space disappears, a quick hop up on the sidewalk, a short spin of the pedals, then a bounce back down to the street takes care of the problem. But with the mass of humanity packed denser than sand on a beach, this option became obsolete.

The Great Joy, though, is the ever mix of cultures perusing up and down the sidewalks infused with the holiday spirit, interconnecting with family and friends in hot pursuit of shopping goals.

Indescribable happiness injects itself, reaching the inner soul, making one glad to be alive. Certain strands in my DNA trigger and I get a seismic uplift in energy when crowds like this gather, massed together for a common cheery purpose.

At these jam points where progress stalled The Fever and I cut over to Rush Street, made progress, and then cut back to Michigan Avenue. A scientist, mapping our cycling pattern, would go nuts, declaring that we ride like dead men. Well, one of us was.

When I arrived at the Hershey's Store at 4 pm, I called each of my siblings to inform them I had to have my bike back by 6 pm sharp. Therefore, I informed them, I needed to leave the Hershey's Store by 5:15 pm. Each assured me we had plenty of time and that they'd be there.

I couldn't resist a Hershey's Hot Fudge Sundae. Taking a bite or two, it sure disappointed me. The ice cream had a grainy, crystallized, almost gritty texture. *Yuk*. The alleged vanilla ice cream didn't taste very vanilla-like, more like bad wet sand. Furthermore they didn't have Hot Fudge Sundaes, only Chocolate Sundaes. How horrifying that the Hershey's Store on Michigan Avenue, in the heart of the Miracle Mile, didn't offer Hot Fudge Sundaes. Tragic—perhaps a Cardinal Sin of the highest scream. I felt small tremors as Milton Hershey turned in his grave.

Pete and Greg arrived together at 4:30 pm. "Geez, they don't even have Hot Fudge," they fussed. "What's the deal with that?"

"The ice cream isn't very good," Pete said. "Hey, as long as we're here why don't we head over to the Hancock Center. We can make it before you have to return your bike."

"No. We don't have time."

"We're already here. We can head over there quick," he said.

I didn't try to hide my irritation when I told him "You don't get it do you? I have to *leave* by 5:15 pm in order to return my bike by 6 pm sharp in order to *not* be charged for another day. It's already ten minutes to five. It takes twenty minutes to just walk over there. Also, we had agreed do get a Hot Fudge Sundae across the street at Ghirardelli's. So no, we can't squeeze in the Hancock Center before I return my bike. You'll have to wait until after I come back."

Pete continued his insistence.

"No!!" I said.

We went round and round, eventually reaching a compromise. I would return the bike and call them after doing so and we would all meet at the Hancock Center.

After returning the bike and taking a bus back north up Michigan Avenue to the Hancock Center, a familiar feeling arose. Time stood still and painful flashbacks played. The infinite stationary parking lot, otherwise known as Michigan Avenue, became the new normal. Road construction couldn't be blamed this time, but holiday congestion could. I concluded walking would have been faster.

After numerous delays we all arrived at the Hancock Center; I-57 BBQ would have to wait for another day. I greeted a red-headed lady working the desk, and said, "I received permission from your director to film at the top. We're honoring a friend of mine who recently died. It's a long story."

"Do you have a lot of equipment?"

"No, just my little Kodak Playsport." I showed it to her.

"I'll have to call my manager. Do you know the name of the person you talked to?" Her uneasiness didn't hide itself.

"No. I'm sorry I don't. If I can get access to the internet I can look up the emails and give you the name. Also, my camera is running out of power. This may sound strange, but can I possibly plug it into the USB port of your computer to recharge it?"

After a short wait an African-American lady arrived on the scene. It was obvious the left hadn't talked to the right. Her face scrunched like the first lady's, and her perplexed replies were a mirror image.

"If I can get internet access I can show you the emails to tell you the name of the director I traded emails with," I said.

"Follow me."

"Oh, and one more thing. Can I possibly plug my camera into the USB port of your computer to recharge it? It ran out of power," I turned an embarrassed shade of red somewhat hidden by the dim shadows of the area.

I got her the name she needed. After that, smooth sailing. When it came time to pay for the tickets, she said, "No charge, this is on me."

"Thank you," I replied, feeling a warm flame of gratitude. I really appreciated her gesture.

The elevator moved at the same blazing speed it did years ago, although the configuration of the observation deck had changed. I searched for the spot where the turnstile stood 20 years ago, where The Fever had refused to go in. We set up shop. Now, The Fever had no choice. He was going in.

"ACTION!" Pete yelled.

My heartbeat and pulse accelerated. I could sense the Déjà Vu. The Fever's spirit reigned down. I emerged from the shadows of the long hallway and walked to the imaginary turnstile, proceeding through it.

I said, "20 years ago, in this very spot, The Fever refused to go in. He's owed me this debt ever since. Now, finally, The Fever is paying his debt to me. Fever, you're going in!"

Walking through, my heartbeat and pulse pumped at an alarming rate. I said, "Fever, you made it! Your debt is paid in full." After making it through I just stood there as the significance finally hit me. I paused, and then slapped high fives with Pete.

Just then my pulse slowed and my heartbeat began to recede. I still continued to process the moment. It almost seemed anti-climactic. After 20 years ... the phone calls, the needling, the exhortations, the begging, and now ... finally.

There wasn't any warm, fuzzy, anti-climactic moment for Pete. He wasted no time slapping high fives back, yelling, "Fever, you did it!"

Greg let loose and slapped high five, too, screaming for all to hear, "Beautiful baby! Beautiful!"

Dancing broke out in the hallway; the celebration steamed ahead. The people nearby didn't know how to react. But they knew something wonderful had just happened. They smiled too and their glow added in ways I can't describe.

It's a weird feeling doing something that's been on the docket for 20 years. Never did I see it playing out like this. No longer would The Fever be indebted to me. But he has to know, I didn't charge interest.

Up in the open air skyway, off came the cover of the little tin container. Out went The Fever to spread his bubbly spirit, bringing good cheer to the fine citizens of Chicago below. I bonded with The Fever's kindred spirit one last time. There wasn't any room for tears, only joy.

Our final act that evening was to book it by taxi to Lou Malnati's Pizzeria on State Street. They came highly recommended and didn't disappoint. The pizza of choice, a large Italian sausage deep dish with onions. A side of cheese bread to boot. That cheese, that sausage, that crust. Oh, my.

Playing the role of Mother Hen, pleading with Pete and Greg, I said, "Imagine we get to the train station a little too late. Imagine the train has left the station and we are stranded 25 miles from our hotel late at night, dark and cold in the middle of downtown Chicago. Imagine the long expensive taxi ride back to the motel, arriving late. Real late. Imagine how much fun it wouldn't be. And expensive. Just imagine."

Their lack of concern for time turned more serious as the vexing hour approached. Constant reminders of the nightmare scenario eventually struck a chord. Possessed, we hailed a taxi with urgency.

"Get us to the train station!" Pete directed the taxi driver, pounding the words with a sharp bite.

Upon arriving at the train station, not forgetting the immortal words of the conductor, we scrambled to purchase return tickets. The train ride back evoked the same pleasant warmness as before, creating another series of *aha* moments.

CHAPTER 14

strike one for the cabbie

On that wet and rainy Saturday in Chicago, I got elected to drive by a landslide. Agendas bubbled over and *we can do it all* became the mantra of the day. Somewhere in the mix, barbeque at I-57 BBQ loomed. Ferrera's Bakery in Little Italy, by unanimous decision, became destination number one.

Trying to find a place by collective consensus is sheer madness. It just doesn't work. No one trusts the map in hand and everyone thinks the directions are bogus. By a strange twist of nature the backseat drivers always know how to get there better than the map.

Exiting the freeway at Taylor Street, Ferrera's was, in theory, between Racine and Western. Cutting through the heart of the University of Chicago at Illinois (UIC), a sprawling campus, Pete waged a tremendous battle to reconcile the map to the GPS directions.

Driving west we went through what we thought was Little Italy, but it seemed too new. Serious doubts rose to the surface. Backseat drivers, impatient Chicago drivers, the constant sound of *honk, honk, honk*, narrow streets, and the innate act of driving itself created a state of far-reaching fatigue, like body blows in boxing.

"Take a right," Pete said.

"No. Go straight farther," Greg said, "Now take a right. Go down a few blocks and take a left, it should be there." *Honk, honk, honk.*

"No. Go straight," Pete added. *Honk, honk, honk.* "Watch out for that car!" *Honk, honk, honk.*

On our second attempt to find Little Italy we couldn't help but notice the street sign screaming, GREEK TOWN.

From the backseat, "Well, shouldn't there be a sign saying 'Little Italy,' just like there is a sign saying, 'Greek Town?'"

I said, "Well, you would think so. Let's look for one." We turned the car around.

"I don't get why they don't have a 'Little Italy' sign like they have a 'Greek Town' sign?"

"I don't know either," I said.

These questions are more than rhetorical. Given I possess an engineering degree, the myth is that I know everything. All people, young and old, male or female, black or white, from the north, south, east or west, upon learning of my degree treat me as the Oracle. They ask a question and wait in complete confidence, trusting that I know the answer. From flashlights to computers to flowers to why the Giant's coach called a certain play, it doesn't matter. To think that I know it all is irrational at best, but nonetheless, I appreciate the flattery.

Stopping at a pizza place, Pete said, "Gregster, go in there and find out where we are." (It's always Pete's idea to send in the Gregster).

"Ok." He reported back that the workers didn't know, and that he "got the evil eye."

A decision was made by the backseat drivers to go south. "I am going to drive and drive and drive until somebody tells me to make a turn. You just tell me where to turn," I said.

The backseat drivers couldn't agree on where to take that turn.

"You know, this doesn't look like a good area of town. I think we are in the heart of South Chicago. Not good. Nothing looks Italian," I said. "All I see are warehouses and manufacturing plants."

Stopping at a gas station, Pete said, "Gregster go in there and find out where we are."

"Ok."

"Why don't you go in there yourself?" I asked.

"Fine," Pete said, in a grumpy tone. He reported back that Little Italy was back near where we had started from.

We got the brilliant idea that instead of relying on GPS or maps or bad directions why not just call Ferrara's and ask for directions. We found out that we hadn't gone far enough west on Taylor Street. We burned through an enormous amount of time following bad leads, bad directions, and going around and around in dizzying circles.

Spotting a Gangster Tour bus, Pete blurted, "Do you see that bus Gregster? We gotta go on that tour. Gregster, let's go."

"Ok."

"We have to stop at Al's. We have to stop there. It was on *Diners, Dives, and Drive Ins*. We have to go there," Pete insisted.

"Ok."

Our map showed that President Obama's Chicago home wasn't far away, Near Hyde Park in South Chicago. This became another spurious addition to an agenda when we hadn't even crossed off the first item yet. And by now it was early afternoon.

Arriving in an area with an old-world charm and seeing businesses with staunch Italian names, we knew we had found Little Italy. Reveling in the ambience of Ferrara's, established in 1908 by Italian immigrants, the variety of the menu and the aromas were almost too much to take. This led to an atmosphere of snarf and swallow, making quick work of Vienna beef sandwiches and classic Italian pastries with elusive names, and Diet Coke, of course.

The sheer beauty of Ferrara's lies in the old-world charm and deep family roots. The owner listened with the patience of an angel to our epic journey. Our cameras came roaring out: *snap, click, tink, click, click,* and *snap.*

LuLu's, another Italian eating establishment with old-world charm, sat right across the street.

"Ribs, they have ribs?" I asked rhetorically upon seeing their sign.

"Are you going to try ribs?" Greg added.

"I want to, I really do, but I am still full. I'm only going to have ribs at I-57."

"Hey, they have ribs." Pete said.

"I know."

"Are you going to try them?"

"No."

If I were to look up fun and friendly in the dictionary, it would show a picture of LuLu employees. Spirited, funny, and humorous with down-home earthiness, it's like we were old friends stopping by.

Mustering up enough appetite to split a Chicago Dog with Greg, it was good, but skinny. Conventional wisdom says that Chicago Dogs are big jumbo-sized dogs with everything on them. The typical tale told by tourists is that a Chicago Dog casts a shadow the size of a football field, and it takes a fleet of forklifts to move, covered in toppings so dense, so heavy, that steel beams crack under the weight.

By contrast, a real Chicago Dog, purchased in Chicago, is by default the skinny dog which I can hold with one hand, loaded with toppings or not. The jumbo size is extra. Ahh, the lessons life teaches us.

Caving in to Pete's demands we pulled in to the tiny parking lot of Al's #1 Dogs. For the record, *Diners, Dives, and Drive Ins* never filmed at Al's, but *Man vs. Food* did.

Across the street stood a fun, colorful lemonade stand, closed for the season. After taking pictures we headed into Demitasse, the coffee shop next door. Independent coffee shops too often look crappy and feel like they cater to the Generation X crowd. The corporate gleam, however, of a Starbucks or Caribou, attracts the inner Yuppie in me and wins out virtually every time.

Demitasse offered a colorful alternative to typical independent crap heaps. It looked average with long and narrow with booths to the left and a bar area to the right. The walls were painted light tannish brown.

The magic lay in the back wall, covered in a mural so cheery our spirits lifted in an abundance of rainbow colors. The other walls weren't left out of the action either, decorated by colorful paintings designed to transmit their own radiance.

We prodded two fun attractive female employees to dispense a treasure trove of history. The 1930s Gangster, John Dillinger, hung out in the Little Italy area of Chicago we were in. During Prohibition he stored liquor in their basement while the place fronted as a Chinese laundry. In the stairwell of the building right next door one of Dillinger's men was shot during a shootout. Wanting more, but forced to leave for the sake of accomplishing agenda items, we headed out, longing in our hearts.

Passing the University of Chicago on the way to Hyde Park, memories of visiting there in years past came to life. John D. Rockefeller put up the funding to start the University. Every building has old-world French European design, making the campus a must-see destination.

Upon entering Hyde Park street names change as though the park is some kind of divine dividing line. The map marked Obama's house so well a blind man could find it. And it was our lucky day. A prominent green arrow pointed to a Presidential Gift Shop in the middle of the park, igniting an ecstatic joy. "We need to go to that shop and buy Obama souvenirs," someone said.

In order to actualize all the agenda items, time became a precious commodity. My list remained fortuitous: A quick stop at the Shedd Aquarium, drive Pete and Greg into downtown for the Gangster Tour, kill time, another quick stop at the Shedd Aquarium, pick up Pete and

Greg, go to I-57, etc., etc. I felt as fried as a depleted tomato; I didn't sign up for this. This day was supposed to be fun and relaxing.

We found Obama's house easily enough just east of Hyde Park. His mansion of a house rests on a short residential block full of mansions. On one end of the block is a set of metal barricades. A large black Secret Service SUV blocked the entrance to the street. It was a scene straight out of the movies. We didn't check to see if they were wearing mirrored sunglasses, but the assumption was that they were.

On the other end of the block was a similar set of barricades. A large sign said RESIDENTS ONLY. Just beyond the barricades sat a black Cadillac which had all the markings of a Secret Service vehicle. Pete insisted (no, argued) there were other large Secret Service black SUVs on the block, but I didn't see any.

We looped back to the first SUV. Greg, ever the tourist that he is, couldn't resist his instincts: "Slow down, slow down. I want to get a picture. Why can't you just stop?"

"NO!"

"Come on. Slow down so I can get a picture. Why can't you just stop?"

"You can't just stop and take pictures of the President's house. What? Do you want to get out and ask the friendly Secret Service fellows if they will pose for a picture? Are you planning on walking up to the house to ask if President Obama and the First Lady might want to share a tea together? Heeeeelllloooooo! He is only the most powerful man in the world and there are bad guys out there!"

"Well, why do they have his house listed on the map then?"

"Just because it is on the map doesn't mean we can walk right up to the door."

Upon Greg's continued insistence we circled the

President's block numerous times, slowing down each time as we approached the imposing black Secret Service SUV. I repeated over and over, "I told you so, I told you so," preparing for the potential doom of flashing lights behind us.

The green arrow on the map showed the Presidential Gift Shop to be in the middle of Hyde Park. Bordering the west side of Hyde Park sits S. Martin Luther King Drive, with S. Cottage Grove Ave. bordering on the east. E. 51st street borders the North while Rainy Dr. cuts a loop through the middle of the park. To add to the confusion, upon turning left from E. 51st street onto S. Martin Luther Dr. the road splits in two with Elsworth Dr. forking to the left, following the inner western boundary of the park. Elsworth Dr. then loops into Rainy Dr. which connects to Payne Dr. which, similar to Elsworth Dr., runs inside the park's eastern boundary, parallel to Cottage Grove Ave. eventually connecting to it. Too much information, I know.

It is important to me, as the driver, to get you to understand how those streets connected to each other. I need your sympathy as I took a veritable pounding from the backseat drivers while attempting to navigate them. They showed no mercy when barking their demanding and insane directions.

To summarize: Elsworth Dr. together with Rainy Dr. And Payne Dr. forms a horseshoe-shaped loop running just inside the border of the park starting at the northwest corner and ending at the northeast corner. Bordering the west side of the park is S. Martin Luther King Dr., while bordering on the east is Cottage Grove Ave. Finally, E. 51st borders the north, and don't forget, Rainy Dr. cuts the park in half. Being good at directions I studied the map with a renewed intensity not seen since my college days.

"Go left, no go straight, get on Elsworth. It's between Elsworth and Payne," Greg said.

I said, "Look, Elsworth splits from Martin Luther King Dr. on the west while Payne parallels Cottage Grove on the east. I have already circled the park a number of times and I don't see the gift shop."

Pete could not wrap his head around the idea that both Martin Luther King Dr. and Elsworth Dr. run parallel on the west side of the park while Cottage Grove Ave. and Payne Dr. run parallel on the east.

"No, the gift shop is between Elsworth and Payne. Get on Elsworth and drive over to Payne," he said.

"We are just going in circles around the park. I have already done that and I don't see the gift shop," blurting the words, on the verge of yelling them.

Greg said, "It's between Elsworth and Payne. Why are you turning on Martin Luther King Drive? No. Don't turn on Cottage Grove. It's between Elsworth and Payne. Why isn't there a sign? There should be a sign. I can't believe it."

Do you agree with me now that I could have used your sympathy then? I circled the park countless more times desperate for a sign or building—anything—that said *Presidential Gift Shop*.

My head hurt something fierce, nearing explosion. No sign. No building. Nothing. A battle raged within, daring me to curse at will. A sign on Rainy Dr., smirking like a neighborhood brat, told those smart enough to read that the DuSable Museum was to the right.

A few times, for fun and revenge, I took a short drive straight west towards a scary-looking area of South Chicago. This did the trick. "Where are we? This doesn't look good," someone would say.

"Nope, can't be here," I'd say smirking and turning around.

At the gas station, even after showing them the map, the attendants were clueless. And so my theory lives on: attendants don't know anything anymore. The times, how they have changed. Those former beacons of rock-solid information are now bankrupt of anything useful to the everyman tourist.

"Hurry up. I have to be downtown at 4:45 pm to make it to the Gangster Tour. Hurry up. Skip this gift shop thing, we gotta get moving," Pete said.

"No, we're already here, I want to see the gift shop," I said. "Why don't we stop at that building we keep seeing?"

"Okaaaay," came the answer with undisguised sarcasm. "We are heading into the DuSable Museum."

"What will it hurt?" I asked.

"Hurry up."

The parking lot was a skinny little thing. Easy to get into, but hard to get out of, requiring a small act of God.

"Hurry up."

"We'll only be a few minutes," Greg said.

The DuSable museum is an African-American museum highlighting famous African-Americans. I said to the clerk, "Excuse me, but we are trying to find the Presidential Gift Shop. See, here it is on this map, but we can't find it. Do you know where it is?"

"We have a gift shop with a few Obama items in it, but we are not a Presidential Gift Shop the way they show it on the map. We are the gift shop they are referring to, but they marked it incorrectly," he said.

Curses.

Trotting down the hall to the gift shop, I bought an Obama mini-biography book and Greg bought a pair of Obama gift sandals. We explained the problem with the map to the clerk behind the counter at the gift shop who listened with intensity, while at the same time modeling patience.

"My brother here wanted me to stop our car so he could get out, walk up to Obama's house, and take pictures," I said to the clerk.

"Think that one through honey. Not possible. Think

it through honey," the clerk said to Greg. She glared straight at him with no smile anywhere. Score.

I puzzled how we could we be so fooled when it was right in front of us the whole time. Looking at the map again, the green arrow labeled *Presidential Gift Shop* pointed to a small black icon numbered 43. Tracking 43 on the map ledger, the DuSable Museum appeared next to the 43.

We ignored the black icon labeled 43 all afternoon to focus only on the green arrow. As they say, If all else fails read the instructions. Another viable option would be for them to make a better map.

Back in the car, Pete stormed a barrage at us, "Hurry up, time is wasting, we gotta get moving." He devised a game plan where I would take them to their destinations, kill time, and then pick them up in reverse order, finally meeting at the McDonald's in downtown.

"I feel like I'm everyone's taxi driver. What about me?" I said. "I should get to have some fun too. I've been driving all day and I'm sick of driving. Why can't you guys take a train or bus or something?"

"What are you doing? Turn there, turn there! You missed the turn! You missed the turn!" Pete charged.

"I know, I know, but I can't change it now, and quit talking. I'm the only driver in here," I said, before eventually making a quick stop at the Shedd Aquarium.

"Turn here, turn here! You missed it, turn left at the next light," Pete hissed. "What are you doing? This is the wrong exit! We're not going to Soldier Field!"

"KNOCK IT OFF!!!," I said, using all the patience skills I ever learned; deep breaths, counting to 10, and visions of happy moments.

I was only too happy to dump my load. No more edicts, please. Enough. Finding a Starbucks coffee shop on the south side of downtown, my evening transformed into a few mellow moments of peaceful bliss.

There is nothing quite like sitting in a comfy chair,

sipping on a delicious hot chocolate, and reading the biography of President Obama for 45 minutes straight. No
barking, no edicts, no demands, no stress, no fatigue. I
became the master of my own destiny once again.

Checking the clock, I hopped up from the chair. "Excuse me, sir. Do you know how to get to Lake Shore Drive
from here?"

"I'm sorry. I don't."

"Thank you." I asked another patron, "Excuse me sir.
Do you know how to get to Lake Shore Drive from here?"

"I'm sorry. I don't."

"Thank you."

Persisting in asking patron after patron in the belief
someone would know produced no fruit, always receiving
a polite, "I'm sorry, I don't."

I eventually took matters into my own hands and
made a skip to the car. I stepped on the accelerator without any plan, believing that if I want it to work out, it
would work out.

Jackson Street appeared a few blocks away. I took a
left and approached Michigan Avenue. It's there a glimmer caught my eye. An innocuous little white and brown
street sign on the right marked something significant.
Squinting, and then squinting again, my heart skipped a
few beats. A familiar silence overtook me. Then, in one
wallop I hauled off and screeched, "*Whooooey, yeeehhaaah, yipppeeee!*" Another victory dance in the car
seat. I was there, *The Mother Road*. Route 66. The Alpha
and the Omega. The Beginning and the End.

After making the return stop at the Shedd Aquarium
in a suitably torrential downpour, I cruised to the agreed
to Rock 'n' Roll McDonald's in the heart of downtown. I
scoffed with indignation when I read the parking lot sign:
$12 for 20 minutes. "Never," I said, and circled until Pete
and Greg showed up.

The hour had arrived. Time for ribs at I-57 BBQ. After playing taxi driver all day and catering to my siblings every whim, it was my turn.

"Isn't it late to be eating ribs?" one of them asked.

"NO! WE ARE GOING TO I-57!"

I-57 gets its name due for the proximity of the original one to the freeway of the same name, right off the 115th street exit. The weather had turned dark, dank and depressing. Rainy too.

"Is this area safe?"

"Don't worry. The online reviews said it's in a safe part of town," I reassured. Closer to 25 miles south of downtown, further than I expected, it was a plain stand-alone building painted a bright fire engine red with an I-57 logo attached to the front. The logo looked like an I-57 interstate sign.

It was take-out only with a steady stream of people ordering our entire time there. Never one for missing an interview, I recruited the young high school age African-American man working behind the bullet proof glass. He gave puzzled looks not seeming to share my enthusiasm. Despite this, he agreed to be on camera.

My siblings' safety concerns were not comforted by the knowledge that this was the only barbeque place I'd ever visited with bullet-proof glass. There was no direct connection between customer and clerk.

Built into the bullet-proof glass was a large metal black box, the size of a small safe, with doors on both ends. When the clerk delivered the food to the customer, he opened the door on his end, placed the food in the box, and closed the door. The customer opened the door on his end, slid the food out, and closed the door. No direct contact.

My brothers' fears were heightened by the fact we were the only white people in there for our entire stay. I've stated before that judgments and assumptions are often made when they shouldn't be. Understand on that late Saturday night sat a band of mild-mannered white suburbanites in a take-out only restaurant in an all-black area of South Chicago, an area with a reputation for crime and violence unmatched, with no other white people in sight. They didn't say it, but I could see the fear.

I-57 does a wham-bam business on a Saturday night. Just when it looked as though the line would stop more people would hop in the door. They offered more menu items than your average barbeque place.

The other customers were all business, the workers, too. Customers would come in, place their order, wait, get their order, and head out the door. No chit-chat. Nothing. We were the most interactive ones there.

We waited for the line to go down and ordered. Pete and Greg shared rib tips and hot links. I ordered a half-slab of ribs. In the mean time we chatted amongst ourselves and I explored a little bit.

A small white church stood across the street, like a dark shadow. Single story, the A-frame door paralleled the shape of the roof. High above the door, facing I-57, hung an unmistakable Cross. I fired up the camera and said, "I've noticed that across the street from I-57 is a church. Maybe some form of Higher Power has blessed their ribs."

Eventually Pete and Greg's order showed up. I had to wait for mine. There were no tables in that small lobby, so we all sat on chairs. It was too cold out, and the idea of eating in the car didn't appeal to us.

At I-57, Christmas must be their favorite time of year for the walls were a bright Santa Clause red with impressively large red white and blue menus hanging on them. Their entire theme was red, red, and more red, like Nebraska football fans. Even a big red number 57 was ingrained into the black rubbery gym-like floor.

Pete and Greg both liked the rib tips better than the hot links. They agreed they were nice and smokey. "The hot sauce is really spectacular," Pete said. "It has a great bite to it; a dynamite aftertaste, really good."

After a 20 minute wait my order came. Bringing it back to where we were sitting and opening it, WOW! That's a half slab? Did they make a mistake? By at least a factor of 2-to-1 the outrageous number of bones outnumbered any other half-slab I've ever eaten. It covered the entire space of the plastic container.

This wasn't some small plastic container you might get at McDonald's to take a Big Mac home in. Uh huh. It was the kind used to take large food items home in, oversized pancakes or a big rib-eye steak, for example. I estimated the container to be ten inches square. That's almost a square foot. Hidden underneath the two-handed half-slab, unseen by the naked eye, were an unconscionable amount of French fries slathered in I-57's own home-made barbeque sauce.

The time had come to interview the worker. The bullet-proof glass made for tough hearing, but we overcame it. "Here I am, Mr. Y. at I-57 Chicago on the Mr. Y. BBQ Tour. I've eaten as many of these ribs as I can. This is ... right? Did I get that right?" leaning up to the glass to hear him.

"Yes," he said, adding a short wave.

"He says hello from I-57. Is it always this busy?"

"Yes, on weekends," he said, leaning closer to the glass since he spoke so softly. "Just on the weekends it's this busy."

"It keeps you on your toes, doesn't it? Alright. Mr. Y. and his BBQ Tour says thank you and have a great evening. Now, back to the ribs (*hiccup*). Well, I ate what I could (*hiccup*). The reason you see this much left is 'cause I'm fu ... (*hiccup*), excuse me, I'm full (*hiccup*), there were so many ribs (*hiccup*), so many ribs, I can't finish every last ounce of meat (*hiccup*), about the best I'm gonna do, tonight (*hiccup*)."

Pete and Greg shared my loot. Pete portrayed the ribs to be *definitely* smokey while I found them to be *somewhat* smokey. He said the sauce was *definitely* tangy while I said it was *somewhat* tangy. We reached a compromise, agreeing the ribs were pleasantly tender.

They weren't the most flavorful ribs ever tasted. Flavorful enough, but not the most ever. However, the place earned an award for the most outrageous portions ever. Each bone by itself was an overly generous portion. Now put it all together into a half-slab and watch out. From a pure taste perspective the French fries were adequate but not earth shattering. In quantity alone they were off the charts.

The red barbeque sauce looked and tasted similar to the red sweet and sour sauce used in Chinese food. It had the same color, quality, texture, and flavor which left me wondering if sweet and sour sauce was a component of the barbeque sauce.

To summarize: The ribs, outrageous. The quantity of French fries, off the charts. The bread, generous. The coleslaw, generous. The dream had come true, and the promise I had made to myself months earlier fulfilled. I-57 BBQ. Check.

We had more agenda items to accomplish. Chicago is famous for their Blues and we weren't about to miss that opportunity. We made a decision to visit the Chicago Blues Bar on the north side, in the Lincoln Park area.

Being a skilled urban driver I drove. "You look like a cabbie the way you are hunched over the wheel. Ha ha ha ha," they laughed. I hunched out of pure survival from fatigue, and racked up 36 miles one way to the Blues Bar.

We arrived in the Lincoln Park area at 10:30 pm. Locating the bar was nearly as difficult as finding a needle in a haystack. After driving straight up Halstead Avenue from downtown it intersected with two other roads, W. Fullerton and N. Lincoln. Being from Minneapolis navigating two intersecting roads is challenging enough. But three? Good God.

I plowed through a large puddle while making a sharp left onto Fullerton. I twisted and turned my head in all directions searching for the bar. In the corner of my eye I caught a glimpse of a woman in a black dress in obvious distress. I heard from the back seat, "*Ha ha ha ha! Whah whah whah whah! Hee hee hee hee! Hoo hoo hoo hoo!*" Laughter seemingly bounced off every crease in the car.

"What are you laughing for? Was it the turn I made?"

Pete said, "When you made the turn you created a tsunami like wave that totally drenched that woman. She was all decked out in an expensive dress and shoes. I *just* rolled the window down because I was going to ask her if I could take her picture. You should have seen the look on her face. It's like she was paralyzed. She didn't move, she just stood there all freaked out. *Ha, ha, ha, ha!* You really got her good."

"Oops, she's not all decked out now. Should I stop and apologize?"

"NO!" Greg screamed. "Don't stop! Keep going."

* * *

The Chicago Blues Bar has been located on N. Lincoln for decades. It's an old-time saloon in the literal sense. A skinny little aisle separates the drinking bar on the right from seating booths on the left.

Blues music, Chicago style, fuses old-time New Orleans Cajun rhythms with the rockabilly thump of the blue hills of Kentucky.

Getting a better view of the band playing the stage along the back wall required reviving old ushering skills. Snaking between the crammed bodies jamming the aisle took every trick of the trade.

"Excuse me, could I squeeze by please?"

Some moved and some refused to budge their inebriated flesh. At these jam points my arms became the jaws of life, prying an opening just enough for me to slide through before the opportunity closed shut. In other cases slithering like a Black Mamba snake did the trick.

The Who's enduring song *Pinball Wizard* describes with great accuracy the manner in which I bounced and bumped like a pinball. Had this been a life size pinball game I would've I racked up points like there's no tomorrow. *Bing, bing, bing;* unstoppable, feeling no pain.

I stood behind a distracting couple for an hour. Not because of their behavior, but just by their being. The woman was attractive—hot is a better word—with dark hair, dark eyes, dark skin (which by its very nature drives me bananas), leaving me to *oogle* and *aaah* in the most immature ways. She couldn't have been more than 25 or 30 years old.

The man, 6 ft. 2 inches looked like a typical white, squeaky clean corporate middle manager in his mid to late 50s. Long-sleeved dress shirt with a collar, short grey hair, white t-shirt underneath (Who wears a t-shirt underneath, really?). I do mean to say his button-down shirt was neatly tucked in, nice looking belt, wearing pressed slacks, with nice shoes to boot.

He never moved from his spot. In this moment I pondered and fussed over proper dating ages. In our conformist society a man and a woman *should* be close in age. Right? *Pooh, pooh.*

What wasn't clear was whether they had just met or come as a couple. They chatted with each other more and more, and over time they got chummier and chummier. Every guy around them tried to act like they weren't paying attention. But like me, they weren't good at it.

She stroked his face over and over, kissing him everywhere. All the patrons drooled. Me too. At one point he slid his arm over her, embracing her tighter and tighter, and playing with her hair in an ever attention-getting way. None of us drooling thought this to be fair.

They had a lot to say to each other, blanking out everyone else. Rather, she never stopped talking, out chatting him by a factor of 5-to-1. I marveled at how she could have so much to say in so short a time. As the night got longer they headed out together, an item. All the rest of us were left to dream.

I spent a short time focusing on the band. A bar worker, an employee of 34 years, stopped to schmooze. His memories were plenty, and he beamed at the ready to share a story on a moment's notice.

In one recollection *The Blues Brothers* actors, Dan Aykroyd and John Belushi, used to frequent the bar. Aykroyd still does. After filming of the movie ended the police car used in it was given to a friend of his. The friend happened to own a pizzeria, and unfortunately died. The family, not knowing what to do with the car, sent it to the junkyard to be crushed into a 1000 little pieces. They didn't know.

Pete, Greg, and I arrived back at the hotel at 1:30 am. Each of us had slept on a bed one night and on a mattress another. To break the tie and decide who got the beds this night I said to Pete, "Pull two names out to see who gets a bed tonight."

"You won," I told him after he drew names. Whooping and hollering he couldn't contain himself. Letting him go on for a while, I finally said, "I have to tell you the truth. You didn't really draw your name. I pulled your leg. You drew me and Greg."

"I want two out of three," he said, contorting his face in a mad, grisly expression.

"No."

"It isn't fair. Greg's not in the room."

"You didn't think it was unfair when you thought your name was drawn. You were whooping and hollering and celebrating. Only after finding out your name wasn't really drawn did you think it wasn't fair. You can't do that. You won the air mattress tonight."

"(*Bleep*). (*Bleep*). This isn't fair. I'm getting screwed. I slept on it last night and it leaked and I'm not doing that again."

"The reason your mattress leaked last night is because I pulled a joke on you. I unscrewed the valve when you were sleeping."

"No you didn't. It had a leak."

"Yes, I did."

Pillows flew through the air in dramatic fashion, headed towards the wall. They crashed with an imperceptible puff, sliding straight down to the floor. I kept fluffing the blankets for a warm night's sleep. I couldn't wait.

CHAPTER 15

last stand

Now that our top priorities were taken care of we were free to roam and explore unrestrained by a rigid agenda. While the day wasn't rainy, it was cloudy and overcast. Perfect for doing nothing useful.

Lincoln Park is impressive in its selection of shops, bars, and restaurants. There's everything a tourist could want, but picking a restaurant proved to be formidable. Pete was fixated on Mexican cuisine while Greg dreamed of shopping.

I begged, "I just want to make everyone aware that if we leave at 5 pm we will get home at 2 am, and I have to get up at 6 am to make it to work by 8 am. I would really, really appreciate it if we could leave at a reasonable time so this doesn't happen. I won't be happy if it does."

"Oh don't worry about it. We have plenty of time and we'll get going early," they assured me.

Pete is great at making million dollar business decisions but he wages war with indecision when making simpler ones. With him at the wheel we drove up Halstead Ave., turned onto Fullerton Ave., and looped around to N. Lincoln Park. And then we did it again, and again, and again. Mind you, we weren't lost.

By consensus we wanted something unique to Chicago. Each time he would drive up to a restaurant, pause, rationalize, and then drive away. For example, he stopped in front of an interesting Italian restaurant that showed potential. We went through a rationalization process, and drove off.

At another place he stopped in front saying, "Gregster, go check it out."

Gregster hopped out, went in, came back and said, "Yeah, looks cool." More rationalization took place and we drove off.

"Should I check out a side street?"

"Yes, Pete, go ahead, check out a side street," I said. That didn't result in any decision making either, just more rationalization.

After repeating this process with debilitating frequency, he finally declared, "We're eating here."

"I thought you wanted something unique to Chicago. This is an American Grill. Not exactly unique," I said. More rationalization occurred and we drove off.

The Gregster lobbied to go to Dillinger's (A Place for Public Enemies). Our mom, when she was alive, swore that as a little girl she saw John Dillinger walking the streets one day near where she grew up in St. Paul, Minnesota.

We discussed it and made a decision. Park by Dillinger's where Pete would go in for a drink, Greg would shop, and I would do whatever. To get into the spirit of that era Pete plopped up to the bar at Dillinger's and downed a pre-prohibition beer served in only nine states.

I made an attempt at mild persuasion, "Hey, we should eat here. I looked at their menu. They mainly have hamburgers and French fries. Dillinger's is certainly unique to Chicago."

"No! I am not eating here. I want Mexican," Pete declared.

"Ok."

I floated around the neighborhood like a butterfly, visiting the Hi-Top Grill and Bar to watch the Minnesota Vikings on TV. I left for a while to search the neighborhood for interesting restaurants, but regrouped back at the Hi-Top, and then left to search some more.

I found it. The restaurant we had been searching for. It had a global menu, regular and organic cuisines, high quality, reasonable prices, clean and contemporary interior, quaint, and a friendly neighborhood staff. It sat directly across the street from the Biograph Theater, the place where Dillinger was shot dead by Melvin Purvis and his G-men; you certainly can't get more unique to Chicago than that. And its nearness to the Biograph kept it within the loose defacto Dillinger theme we pursued; the pot of gold at the end of the rainbow, the treasure we had been seeking all day.

Scrambling to hit the buttons on my phone, I placed a call, *ring, ring, ring*.

"Hello," Greg answered.

"Gregster. I found it. The unique restaurant we've been looking for. It's right across the street from the Biograph Theater, only a couple of blocks from Dillinger's. Let's eat there." I'm sure he struggled to understand me because I spit it out quick.

"Cool. Sure, we can do that."

"Great, I'll call Pete and let him know. You're really going to like it. Quaint, a big menu to choose from, clean, and it's totally unique to Chicago. It has something for everyone."

"Wow, this Lincoln Park area sure has cool shops," he said. "They had this one shop that had _____ (fill in the blank). Then I went to this other shop, it was really cool, they had _____ (fill in the blank). I want to go to this shop because they have _____ (fill in the blank)."

"Hello. Hello," I said. "Do you want to go to this restaurant? It's called the Zig Zag. It's really unique."

"Sure," Greg said, his tone drifting. "They have really cool shops here." He got a second wind, "I could spend two days window shopping. I wish I had more money. I want to buy _____ (fill in the blank), and man it is so fun here and full of energy."

"Well, do you want to meet there?"

"Sure," he said, back to a drifting tone, "I'll meet you there. Hey I gotta go, there are more shops I want to go look at. Bye."

I punched the buttons on my phone with a fury, placing another call, *ring, ring, ring.*

"Hello," Pete answered.

"Petester, I found this really cool restaurant called the Zig Zag. It's only a couple of blocks from Dillinger's. We should meet there. Greg is all enthused about it."

Pause. "Yeah, I'll meet you there. I'll be there in a few minutes."

"Ok."

A few minutes later, sure enough, the Petester came walking down the street.

"Hey Petester, I found a place where we can eat. It has everything; it's unique and fun, and even has great food choices too. It's right here and it's called the Zig Zag."

"No! I'm not interested. I want Mexican." He didn't even slow down as he passed me. I not even sure he looked at me. Nor did he ask inquisitive questions wanting to learn more.

I had found a gold mine of culinary pleasure. It had all the criteria we said we wanted, and was as unique to Chicago as a place can be. It had win-win written all over it. But in the end, I was rejected and pushed aside by my own kind.

All of a sudden from behind me I heard the Petester yell, "TIMSTER, DID YOU KNOW THE BIOGRAPH IS WHERE DILLINGER WAS SHOT? WE CAME HERE LAST NIGHT ON THE GANGSTER TOUR. THIS IS WHERE HE WAS SHOT!!" He had to have used every ounce of breath in his lungs, making sure I and the rest of the neighborhood heard him.

Turning around. I said, "Oh, I didn't know. Really?"

I chased after the Gregster. We had to do it—make a

documentary. I developed a defacto storyboard and script right there on the fly. I would be the director and host. He would be the cinematographer and lead actor.

"ACTION!" I yelled, like a real Hollywood director brandishing a megaphone. The Gregster worked the camera, my Kodak Playsport.

"Did you know," I asked, walking out the doors of the theater to the street, "that John Dillinger walked out of the Biograph Theater on that fateful night, like I'm doing right now, and took a left out the door." I made a left like Dillinger did and stepped up the pace. "And as he was walking, he became suspicious." I lowered my head in suspicion and peered across the street looking for G-men. "Keep up with me Gregster," who kept pace and shot different angles with zoom-ins and zoom-outs.

"Soon," I continued, "Dillinger's suspicions became a reality. G-Men, led by Melvin Purvis, laid a trap." I continued to walk. "Gun fire erupted, lighting up the night sky. Chaos and bullets rained down. Crowds of movie goers ran for their life." I stopped and pointed, "Dillinger's life ended right where I'm standing, shot dead in the alley." Ironically, right next to the modern day Mexican restaurant where the Petester was eating.

"CUT! Ok, Gregster, keep up. Why don't you lie down right here in the alley like Dillinger's body, after it got shot up with bullet holes."

"Well, it's kind of wet. There's a big puddle there."

"Ok, fine. It's wet. We'll just film where his body lay. Wow, that's a big puddle. Nuts."

"ACTION!" I yelled. "Right here where I'm standing, Dillinger's life ended. His lifeless body was right where this puddle is. CUT! Great job Gregster, great job. I can't wait to see the raw video."

"Me too, man. I want to see it. Let me know when I can see it."

We parted ways and I once again roamed the streets

of Lincoln Park, heading back to the Hi-Top to watch more football games.

Greg and Pete, pushing the Dillinger theme, headed to John Barleycorn's. It's a turn-of-the century bar and a favorite of Dillinger's. He used to buy customers a round of drinks after a big heist. It still has that same old-world charm, but with modern conveniences like big flat panel TVs.

I joined them there and the three of us headed across the street to Starbucks. For the first time this day we were together. Our plan to eat together had bombed in spectacular fashion—great on paper, but the truth is, no one cared.

A small lesson learned on that afternoon is that Lincoln Park has everything a gushing tourist could ever want: shops, restaurants, bars, everything, all nestled neatly together into one compact, dense neighborhood. It's like going to a garage sale, buying a painting for $10, and finding out it's worth millions.

Halligan's Bar, our final act on that breezy afternoon of fun and adventure, was a sports bar in the truest sense. Bears fans stuffed every nook and cranny leaving no wiggle room to roam.

The Bears Faithful decked out in colorful outfits that gave the bar a festive mood while staying true to their loyalties. They were nothing but fun, offering us down-to-earth neighborhood friendliness, even though we were the enemy from Minneapolis.

Anytime the Bears scored a point the place erupted with the Bears Faithful jumping up and down, beer glasses in the air, singing a Bears victory song in unison at the top of their lungs with the familiar refrain, "DA BEARS! DA BEARS!"

"Would you mind if I filmed you guys whooping it up?"

"Go for it man! WHOOOH, YEAAAAHH, GOOOOOO BEEEAAARRRSS!!! DA BEARS! DA

BEARS!" the guy dressed in Bears candy stripes said, slapping high fives with anyone around.

With them celebrating anything that moved, and us celebrating them, it matched the intensity and decibel levels of The Fever going through the turnstiles. With the whooping, clapping, cheering, and yelling in full swing and not ending anytime soon, our time had come to depart. A fitting end to a fantastic afternoon in the heart of one of Chicago's most intriguing neighborhoods.

While it seems like I may have given a faceless, generic, boring list of agenda items accomplished during our Sunday afternoon, and for that matter our entire trip, I assure you I did not. Instead, it illustrates how we brought the hammer down on anything that could be considered predictable.

From the outset our trip was to be an outflow of our happy family personae. Yet, in reality, we each went our separate ways following our own individual hearts. At the same time we interacted together in mysterious concert, in ways not visible to the naked eye or in agreement with human intuition.

In simple terms we gave practical application to the Chaos Theory, which states that things appearing random frequently have an underlying order. Examples often cited are stock market crashes. Go look for yourself. In the end they follow a certain repeatable pattern.

Please examine the particulars of our trip. Use the events of our Sunday afternoon as your scientific data. We followed a single chaotic pattern containing a neat, underlying order. The single repeating pattern is that we had fun. A few hiccups here, a few cat fights there. Who cares? In the end the Chaos Theory, based on questionable science, confirmed the fun we had together. That's what matters. Life is not a straight line, you have to agree.

We had one more important destination before leaving Chicago. We toyed with the idea of skipping it, but none of us had the willpower not to go. Pete punched the destination into his GPS and a few moments later we were on our way to the place we had been salivating over from the get go: MUSTARD'S LAST STAND, billed as *the best hot dog stand in Chicago* by his friend, a Chicago native.

A hole in the wall, opened in 1969, it's on the campus of Northwestern University. It had a plain white exterior mixed with a red angled roof, with big red letters on a yellow sign to boot.

It's small on the inside, no exaggeration here, with the ordering counter to the left and a plain red sit-down bar to the right. The aroma of hot dogs and onions saturated the air, and a timeline of pictures from its 40-plus years of existence populated the wall above the sit-down bar.

All of us ordered Chicago Dogs. I paid extra and went straight for the Jumbo. I wanted the full experience so I added French fries and a Diet Coke too.

"How far is the football stadium?"

"Look out the window" the server said.

We peered out and sure enough 60 feet away, maybe, sat the football stadium.

"Wow, you guys must do a wham-bam business during football games."

"You should have been here yesterday during the football game. It was wall-to-wall people with a line out the door. We have stands all over, too."

Back in the day the owners had a booth at a Custer Festival and got to bouncing ideas for a name for their new business when an idea struck. Why not play off the Custer name? The result, MUSTARD'S LAST STAND. Ingenious and unforgettable at the same time, it rolls smooth off the tongue.

By the time Pete bought a t-shirt and we bid our farewells, it approached 6:45 pm.

"We'll get home at 2 am. Thanks a lot," I said, exhibiting a great attempt at calm.

"Well, we had fun. It was worth it."

On the drive back to Minneapolis I sneezed and coughed, *Aaaahhh chooooo. Aaaahhh chooooo.*

"Give me your straw. I need something to chew on while I drive," Pete said, being a dictator.

"You don't want my straw; I've been sneezing and coughing."

"I don't care, give it to me," he demanded.

We had smooth sailing all the way home. I plopped down to bed at 2 am, got up at 6:15 am, and staggered off to work.

On that Monday a cold came on. On Tuesday night it struck with full fury. On Wednesday I got sent home from work and lay in bed in agony, missing three days of work, but taking three full weeks to recover; sinus infection, chest cold, virus, the whole enchilada.

Pete stopped by on Friday. "Geez I caught something, I was really out of it. I was really wasted on Monday and I could barely function. By Wednesday I was in bed all day. I blame it on you because I sucked on your straw."

I lifted my head up from the pillow and said, "I warned you. I did. I told you I was getting sick and you said you didn't care. Too bad." My voice was filled with raspy, agonizing, stuffy, nasally tones. I put my head back down on the pillow and went to sleep. Sometimes dumb dumb, it's wise to listen to the younger brother.

CHAPTER 16

there i am

The plane set down with a gentle thud on the runway at Los Angeles International airport (LAX) at 11:15 pm California time. At midnight I checked into the Santa Monica Youth Hostel, a stone's throw from the Santa Monica Pier.

I was in the throes of another curveball. Something I didn't see coming. At a moment's notice I had gathered my things, purchased an airline ticket, and was off. Unlike before this curveball was of the good kind, and had nothing to do with barbeque. I left anyway. I warned of diversions.

But I couldn't ignore barbeque. It lurked in the depths of my subconscious. During the intermittent days, preoccupied with getting out there, an idea emerged: add Los Angeles to the Mr. Y. BBQ Tour. Why not? Wouldn't you? The desire, the need, for barbeque didn't disappear. Before leaving I did my homework, doing an internet search. The results were interesting.

Getting up Tuesday morning the drive downtown went smooth. At home in Minneapolis I prepaid for parking at the GottaPark lot near Staples Center. Finding it was another matter. The problem with choosing another lot for $5 all day was their sign that read, MUST BE OUT BY 5 PM. "Where is the GottaPark lot? My map says is should be on this corner," I asked the attendant.

He looked around for a little bit, pondering his answer. "You go across street and you look left, you check on left. Look for ramp."

Rather than going in circles I parked at the West Gate Garage across the street from the Los Angeles Convention Center. It's massive. Each level is the size of a football field, and well-organized.

But something seemed strange. It took a while to figure it out. The ramp was squeaky clean and brighter than sunshine, while most other ramps are dark and dingy and dirt hides in every corner. Normally my pupils open full bore when driving into a normal ramp from lack of light of any kind. Caution is required at every second to not scrape a wall or nick the car. But none of those concerns applied to this ramp. Spacious, clean, well lit, and with extra helpful workers. I parked in space 617 on level P2.

* * *

I crossed the street to the Convention Center and was just about to enter the long stretch of humanity when a twentysomthing worker greeted me. Her reassurance countered my worry, "You'll be fine. Go ahead and get in line."

After stepping in line a voice with a hint of road rage interrupted the celebration, "This is the front of the line. You have to get in the back of the line. It's around the corner."

"Sorry, I didn't know."

Down around the corner, at the end of the line, another smiling pleasant worker asked, "Can I see your voucher please?" She grabbed it, marked it, and certified it.

"Wow, the line isn't that long," I said to myself out loud. "There are maybe only 1000 people in front of me."

"More like 300," replied a voice with an unmistakable British accent. The couple in front, originating from England, but now residing in California, were attending their first American Idol Finale, too. Behind me were college students from San Francisco, making the five-hour drive earlier that morning.

In these small moments, trivial in the everyday experience, bonds are made that are remembered for a lifetime. Everyone has a story to tell, and that's what made the experience whole. The electricity of the moment, the forming of our common purpose, transformed the line into a living breathing organism that couldn't be replicated anywhere else.

Though conversations started out unique to each person, more often than not my conversations with others ended the same: "Wow, you're from Minnesota and you came all the way for this?" They turned to their friend or spouse and repeated, "Do you know he came all the way from Minnesota for Idol? He found out Friday and arrived last night."

That person stood silent, if not stunned, processing what had been heard. And then turned to the person next to them. "Do you know he came all the way from Minnesota for Idol?" And so on. Andy Warhol says we each have 15 minutes of fame, and this became mine.

Soon, conversations were interrupted. "Anyone sitting in a chair get up and grab your chair. We are moving the line. We are going to start handing out tickets. This line *will* be moving forward." The booming voice shook the leaves off the trees. "If you have a chair, now would be the time to grab it."

The line moved at a steady pace and stopped at the corner of LA Live Way and Chick Hearns Ct. A sign rested up against the street pole, reading *American Idol Parking for Green Lot*. I grabbed it.

"Excuse me, would you mind taking my picture?" I asked the nearest bystander, positioning the sign with the Nokia Theater in the background.

"Sure." *Click.*

"Would you mind taking our picture with the sign, too?" a bystander asked, grabbing the same sign.

"Sure." *Click.*

"Us too?" asked another bystander, grabbing the sign.

"Sure." *Click.*

The domino effect of the sign passing from by-stander to bystander increased to frenzied proportions, like when a body is passed from person-to-person at a rock concert.

When I reached the front of the line an Idol worker replaced the voucher in my hand with an actual ticket to the show. Hallelujah! I was in.

Making a poster is not as easy as it looks, and takes a great deal of creativity and coordination. I had supplies splattering every inch of the white rental car trunk. Glue, sparkles, stars, letters, ribbons, blinking lights, anything and everything necessary for the creative process.

I rooted for Jessica Sanchez. Do I focus on her pic-ture or focus on the letters spelling her name? What shapes do I use? Stars only? A combination of stars and arrows? Hearts? I don't want to be too sappy. Do I make the arrows point to her picture or her name? Should I use a lot of the red, white, and blue ribbon? Or only a little bit? Do I put ribbon everywhere? Or a smaller piece un-der her picture and nowhere else? I needed to make a statement, but decisions were tough to come by.

Idol fans strolled by during my poster-making process. The same familiar conversation kept taking place.

"Where are you from?"

"Minnesota."

"Wow! You came all the way from Minnesota to see American Idol?"

"Yep."

"That's amazing!" They turned to their friends, "Did you know he is from Minnesota? He came all the way out here to see Idol. He found out Friday he got tickets and now he is here." Over time I developed an ego. My ever-increasing celebrity status afforded a strut to my swagger. I was somebody now.

A group of Hispanic women and their daughters hopped out of a White Ford Explorer. "Excuse me, would you mind taking my picture?" I said.

"Sure ... wow, you're from Minnesota ... we're from San Diego ... we're rooting for Jessica ... you should put on your poster you are from Minnesota." And then seeing the stuff on my poster one of the women said, "Oh, those blinking lights will get you on TV. They will love that. That will get you on TV for sure." Her friends agreed.

* * *

The L.A. Live Entertainment District sits on the southwest corner of downtown Los Angeles. The street, LA Live Way, runs right down the middle of the District. Placing the West Gate ramp in the 9 o'clock position and going in a clockwise direction, Nokia Theater sits at high noon. Across the street from the Nokia theater sits the Staples Center in the 2 o'clock position while the L.A. Convention Center sits at 4 o'clock. This convenience made for easy schmoozing, interrupted by runs back to the car.

In the parking ramp groups hovered around orange traffic cones marking the stalls. They jumped up and down like little kids, yelling, squealing, and snapping pictures. They would run to a cone, squeal, jump, snap a picture, then run to another cone and proceed to squeal, jump, snap a picture, then off to the next cone for the same thing.

What's all the excitement? My curiosity was rising. On each of these cones was an American Idol sign with the name of a famous celebrity on it. Rihanna, Reba McIntyre, Neil Diamond, Scotty McCreery, and Miley Cyrus to name a few.

Soon, I ran to a cone, squealed, jumped, snapped a picture, and then took off to the next cone. Security guards came and shooed all of us away, but not before I got a picture by Jennifer Lopez's cone. Aerosmith's, too. What a rush.

The party started up on the street. Bright sun made the neon green of my poster stand out from afar.

"GO JESSICA, GO JESSICA," a passerby screamed.

"JESSICA! JESSICA! JESSICA!" I screamed back at the top of my lungs.

"JESSICA. WHOOOH! GO JESSICA!" they screamed again, adding for good measure, "MINNE-SOTA, GO MINNESOTA!"

I had never been a celebrity before. In the past I've made a few cameo appearances in my own school videos, for which fellow workers hooted and hollered, but it was nothing compared to this.

I can see why famous Hollywood celebrities wear swanky sunglasses and eat exotic foods. The attention is addicting. It gave me a sense of superiority. I kept honing my strut. I wasn't happy with just my 15 minutes of fame, now I wanted 16.

The Nokia Theater sits on the west side of the plaza while Wolfgang Puck Bar & Grill borders the north end. Not to be left out, the ESPN Sports bar and restaurant borders the east side. A large white tent and an adjacent fenced off press area occupied most of the plaza.

Bright lights attached to framework looked down on the press area. They looked like a row of old gutted out cathode ray tube TVs, with white cloth covering the fronts to diffuse light. It seemed weird, having a bank of lights illuminating an area when bright, glaring, rays of the sun do just fine.

Crowds filled the plaza, jammed up against the fence, hooting and hollering like caged animals—a free for all. My celebrity showed no signs of slowing down. "Are you really from Minnesota? You came all this way to see the show? Do you have tickets? How did you get tickets?" Idol fans asked.

"Yes, I came all this way from Minnesota. I found out Friday afternoon that I got a voucher for tonight's show. I arrived last night," I said. My ego beamed even more and I poised myself to sign an autograph or two. Nobody asked for one, but they did leave with a starstruck look in their eyes.

Over on the Wolfgang Puck side of the fence the crowd moved in a swift motion towards something, like a school of fish. The pulse and pace picked up. The din changed to a roar. I darted toward the action.

Elise Testone, voted off contestant five, walked through the crowd with her dad wearing her trademark small brown fedora. Her cover of Led Zeppelin's *Whole Lotta Love* set the Idol world on fire. It became her signature and most memorable moment on the show.

Person after person stampeded after her, "Elise, can I get a picture of you?" She accommodated everyone. "Elise, can I get a picture of you and your dad?" Each person shoving and pleading, "Elise, please ... dad, can I get your picture, please," begging.

Her dad smiled, "She's the one you want."

"Elise, Elise, please, can I get your picture?" *Snap, snap, snap.* She turned to walk away with her dad. Over the years I've learned to be pushy.

"Elise, can I get my picture taken with you?" I asked, using a sharp tone. Not mean, but direct, similar to a tone I might use to get a student's attention.

"Sure" she said, coming back toward me.

She stood next to me smiling. I whispered in her ear, "You know your song, *Whole Lotta Love*? I used it in a school video I made. Everybody really liked it."

"That's cool, that's really cool," she said.

"I'm sorry you got voted off, I really liked you."

"I'm ok, I'm ok, I'm doing well." She seemed apologetic. Smiling, she left with her dad. Her grace and humility reinforced what I already knew: she's a class act.

Buzzing around the plaza were reporters from every corner of the globe: Asia, West Coast, East coast, Latin America, Europe, Phillip Phillip's home town, everywhere. Male and female, all races, all heritages, decked in their finest clothes, competing with each other to get the next big story. They roamed like lions hungry for prey. Cameras were everywhere: big cameras, small cameras, hand-held cameras, on tripods, on shoulders, aimed in every direction.

Emboldened with a turbocharged ego and driven by an addiction to celebrity, I did what I had to do to get my 16 minutes of fame. Seeing an Asian reporter doing an interview, I thrust my poster towards the camera with all intents of butting in. Good for me, I thought, he took the bait.

"What your name?"

"Tim."

"Where you from?"

"Minnesota." A big smile stretched across his face and his eyes lit up, confident he had the next big interview, with visions of soaring ratings, a promotion, and a meteoric rise in fame.

"Wow. You come long ways."

"Yes. I found out Friday I got a ticket and arrived last night."

Turning to a young Phillip Phillips fan he attempted to create an epic struggle. He asked the young fan, "Why is Phillip going to win?"

"He is such an artist and unique. Everybody loves him," the fan replied.

The reporter persisted. "What are you going to do if Jessica wins?"

"Phillip is going to win," the fan said.

"How about you? What will you do if Phillip wins?" the reporter said, looking at me.

194

"He's not going to. Jessica is going to win," I said, smooth and confident. "I have no doubt. She's the best! She has an incredible voice that no one can match. Did I mention she's only 16?"

The reporter persisted, "One of you for Phillip and other for Jessica. So you argue who best."

"Maybe only debate," I said, not falling for his trap.

"Ok, I point camera at you, and you give big cheer," he said to the little tyke, trying his darndest to create a divide.

"WHHOOOEY, YEEEHAH, GO PHILLIP!" the little tyke said, doing the best his age would allow.

"Ok, now you give big cheer for Jessica."

Taking a few seconds to ready myself, I sucked in oxygen like a deep-ocean diver, planted my feet firmly on the ground, crouched my back, clenched my fists, angled my head slightly skyward, and exploded, thrusting my chest forward.

I unloaded a fury, blasting out the decibels and leaving the little tyke's honest attempt in the rear view mirror. "YIPPEE, GO JESSICA, WHOOYEEE, GO JESSICA, YEAAHHH, JESSICA SANITIZE, WHOOOO!" He didn't have a chance. Only a deaf person would have failed to hear me during that moment of insanity. The reporter reared back and laughed a hearty laugh. He knew he had it: the interview of the century. A good day's work.

Wow I'm really popular, I thought. Those Asian reporters sure like me. I think he was from Japan. I'm nothing here in the United States. I bet if I took a trip to Japan, the second I set down in Tokyo, I'd be mobbed. I'm probably a huge celebrity over there by now and don't even know it. Yeah, I'm probably a celebrity!

The need to eat made rising demands, but it wasn't barbeque that would cure my incurable cravings. A hamburger and fries at the ESPN Sports Bar did the trick. Too much excitement, too much getting caught up in the moment sidetracked my hidden agenda. Barbeque would have to wait, but not go away.

Whenever the cameras from the press area panned the crowd, the party atmosphere exploded in intensity, like a hurricane increasing from category 4 to category 5. In the midst of all the whooping, yelling, and screaming every Idol fan who ever had a sign thrust it forward for the world to see. A battle raged, and the cameras were willing participants.

"You know those two reporters who interviewed me? They're *big time* reporters from Fox Entertainment. Trust me. They're *big*," an Idol fan said.

"Ok, I wouldn't know, I never watch Fox Entertainment. I don't have a clue who they are. If you say they are big, then they are big," I said.

"Trust me, they're *big*."

What am I doing, I thought, I need to be wearing my hip colorful clothes. The Idol voucher said fans need to wear hip, colorful clothes. I'm not a fashion king, so before the trip I turned to my students to save me. I took them on a community outing to the mall and they picked out my clothes. They did a brilliant job, picking tan khaki pants and a short sleeve button down teal shirt adorned with a checkered pattern.

On the way back to the car to change I exchanged whoops and yells with other fame seekers. I couldn't shake this addiction to celebrity. One couple I exchanged whoops with made it known they were from Minnesota too, Blaine to be exact.

A pause hung in the air. I didn't hold back. Soon, I screamed my little Nordic lungs out. "GO MINNESOTA, GO MINNESOTA, WHOA, YEAH, GO MINNESOTA!!!"

Part of the fun is seeing how the other half lived. I strolled through the parking ramp and took note of the cars parked in the stalls. The list of high roller cars would impress any, and I do mean any, Midwesterner on a visit to L.A.

But not me. My rich great aunt and uncle, God bless their souls, lived in a Hollywood mansion in Beverly Hills when they were alive; five car garage, Rolls-Royces, maids, butlers, the works. Back in the late 70s they sold it for $1.5 million and moved into a $2 million ocean front home in Hawaii.

A quick check now in the parking ramp turned up a silver Rolls-Royce, high end BMW, Ford Focus, and Maserati. I'm sure the Ford Focus must have been a mistake for those populate the school parking lot I work at.

In another row sat a gleaming Chevy Silverado pickup truck, a high end Mercedes-Benz, and a top of the line black Rolls-Royce. The guy hand-washing the Mercedes-Benz added a nice touch. The cone on that stall read RANDY JACKSON.

Out on the plaza a female reporter said to a fan, "I'm a reporter from Phillip Phillips' home town. I see you are a Phillip Phillips fan. Tell me why you like Phillip Phillips."

"Well," the fan paused a second, "he is so unique and he makes the songs his own."

Later, I overheard the fan say to a friend, "Wow, I feel so natural. I couldn't think of a good answer about why I liked Phillip Phillips. What's a better answer?"

"Oh, you just tell them that he is a unique artist who brings creativity and soul to the stage in a way that hasn't been seen in 40 years," the friend said.

The fan practiced, "Phillip Phillips is a unique artist who brings creativity and soul to the stage that hasn't been seen in a long, long time."

The friend interjected, "No, no, no. You have to give them a number, something dramatic. Use 40 or 50 years. You have to give them a specific number. It has to be a long time, something dramatic."

The fan practiced again, "Phillip Phillips is a unique artist who brings creativity and soul to the stage in a way that hasn't been seen in 40 years."

"Perfect. Perfect," the friend said, smiling.

Back at the press area the cameras focused on the crowd again. This triggered a mini-stampede where the masses rushing to the fence crushed the masses already up against the fence. In silence each fame seeker prayed an agent would see them and pursue with abandon, contract in hand.

"Did you see that cameraman? He got out his *own* camera and was taking pictures of our signs," one addict to celebrity said to me.

"Yes, I did. Fame has gotta be near."

CHAPTER 17

three, two, one, live

It's weird attending a show live that I have seen a hundred times on TV. Walking into the Nokia Theater the colorful blue, white, and silver hues were overwhelming, giving it the feel of a sci-fi set.

The hardest-working person on the planet is the pre-show host who pumps up the crowd: "IF YOU WANT TO GET ON TV THEN GO CRAZY, GO WILD. KEEP CHEERING LOUD. HOLD UP YOUR SIGNS. GO NUTS. THE CAMERA WILL FIND YOU!!" He worked himself into a lather explaining this.

Commercial breaks are three minutes long, though on TV they seem much shorter. A gentle female voice comes over the auditorium speakers during the breaks saying "Ok, two-minutes-forty-five-seconds ... ok, two-minutes ... ok, thirty-seconds to live ... ten, nine, eight ... one ... we are live."

Ryan Seacrest and the judges don't seem like they do as much during a live show as it appears they do on TV. Same for the contestants. They work hard, but not as hard as it looks on TV.

During breaks a team of makeup people come out and work on the judges. Randy doesn't need his hair worked on, but they sure pat him down good so he doesn't sweat. Like overwhelmed worker bees, other teams of workers change out the stage. Anything and everything significant happens during this time.

The pre-show host works hard during the breaks, never letting anyone forget he is there: "OK, WHEN

RYAN COMES OUT DON'T MAKE ANY NOISE. AFTER HE SAYS (*blah, blah, blah*) THEN LET IT LOOSE. SCREAM. HOLLER. MAKE SOME NOISE. DON'T HOLD BACK!"

On TV everything is so dramatic. Live, not so dramatic. The big screens on the side offer a better view than the live upfront action. I didn't want to sit like mild-mannered Clark Kent. So I did all the host advised us to do: screaming, stomping, yelling, cheering, clapping, waving, standing, turning, and going nuts. I worked myself into a frenzy, sweating like after a yoga workout, thrusting my poster high into the air with ill regard.

In doing so, the couple behind me became annoyed. Despite this I was able to strike up a conversation with them. I learned that they too heralded from Minneapolis, and their son worked for American Idol doing a job on stage. Upon learning they're from Minneapolis, remorse and guilt took hold. I couldn't bear the pressure of dissing a neighbor.

One disagreeable feature of American Idol is that a separate unique song is written for each of the two final contestants, which they sing during the finale. Whichever contestant wins, that song is released as his or her first single.

Phillip Phillips killed it with his song, *Home*. Jessica Sanchez, not so much. The audience sensed it right away. For him, they cheered and clapped like there was no tomorrow. For her, only some modest claps and restrained cheers.

After the show I headed back to the hostel in Santa Monica. I headed down to the Pier before winding down for the night.

I sensed something right away. "Wait, what's this?" I said out loud. My exhilaration bubbled. I put two and two together, "A Route 66 kiosk. Route 66 ends at the Pier! YAHOOOH YEEEHHAAAA!!" I broke into another victory dance, leaving skid marks.

I hustled up to the kiosk to initiate the schmoozing process, I told the clerk, "I've been on stretches of Route 66 before. I saw the sign in Chicago where it starts. I went on a piece of it in Dwight, Illinois, and parts of it in Springfield, too. It was so cool."

"I'm leaving in a few weeks to travel the entire stretch of Route 66," he said. "All of our products are either manufactured right on or within a mile of Route 66."

Seeing it, wanting it, gotta have it, I tore into my pocket scrambling for cash. What my eyes had seen and my thirst desired was an authentic Route 66 Root Beer. The Alpha and the Omega. The Beginning and the End.

CHAPTER 18

you have to do it

The beauty of staying at a youth hostel is the global opportunity to meet and schmooze. I get bolder and take more risks, transforming. I met a woman from Argentina the night before and I couldn't resist the urge to talk to her some more; I had designs on getting her number. This occupied breakfast, but one more thing remained before heading out.

Ring, ring, ring. "Hello, thank you for calling Paramount Studios. How can I help you?" the lady on the phone said.

"Yes, I just bought a ticket to your Studio Tour seconds ago online and discovered I made a mistake and am unable to go. Can I cancel my ticket? I bought it just seconds ago online."

"Sure, give me a minute," she said, warm and pleasant while putting me on hold. After a long monotonous wait she came back on line. "We don't give refunds." She said it terse and business-like.

It took a few seconds for it to register. "Oh, crap. No refunds at all?"

"We don't offer refunds." She remained firm and unbending.

"Well, ok, thank you. Bye."

I headed up to the computer lab with lingering anger, and punched up Facebook. I had those fingers slamming letters on the keyboard in no time. I *knew* my typing class in high school would pay off some day. I let the world know what demons Paramount Studios were for denying me a simple refund. This will teach you, I thought. In the world of social media, you're going down!

Done with venting my anger, I pedaled my rental bike down to the pier. The gate on the Route 66 kiosk was closed. "What time do they open up?" I asked the hot dog vendor next to the kiosk.

"It depends. He should be here by 11 am."

When I made the decision at 10:32 am to head towards Venice Beach, a brilliant idea presented itself; hold the camera in one hand and steer the bike with the other.

While pedaling along the path, I passed a man doing what I've seen no man do before. How is he able to do all that without crashing? I'm jealous. I want to multitask like that.

He possessed tanned weather-beaten skin, decked out in a grey fisherman's hat slightly tilted to the side. He reminded me of the Santiago character in *The Old Man and the Sea*, a book I last read in high school. To finish off the attire—a long-sleeve grey and white-collared shirt with small squares and olive cargo shorts.

His clothes looked old and wrinkled, in need of a wash. The old dirty Adidas tennis shoes on the feet were overshadowed by the bleached white of his athletic socks.

The contraption he rode vertically looked liked some sort of hybrid between a health club elliptical machine and a recombinant bicycle, except in reverse. It had two smaller front wheels and one larger rear wheel with a confounding metal box and a walkie talkie attached to the front frame.

To power the contraption he mimicked the actions of a health club freak. Each arm worked a vertical bar, forward and back, like a cross country skier. Each foot up and down, back and forth, moving in opposite directions.

But true admiration lay in his passenger. Peering out from the basket on the back were two small marble-like brown eyes, locked in a stare with me that warmed the heart. Its tiny white doggie paw stuck out over the side of the basket ready to greet any passerby in need of a warm fluffy friend with floppy ears.

The man with the wrinkled clothes, working the contraption, clutched a leash in his right hand. I followed the leash down to the pavement. A tiny dog, tan in color, trotted along without a care in the world, unaware or unimpressed that his master had perfected the art of multitasking. *Where else but here would I ever see this?* The most I can do is film in one hand and steer with the other.

A few minutes later an elderly gentleman biked at a steady pace along the path. Wearing a white fedora hat with a dark brown band, he had short whitish-grey hair and a full gray seaman's beard. I got ready to ask him about his thinking behind *The Old Man and the Sea*, but abandoned the idea. I figured he was too young to be Ernest Hemingway, who isn't alive anymore anyway.

Owning the look of that famous author, sunglasses attached to a strap hung around his neck. His orange button-down collared shirt and white shorts blended beautifully, if not mystical, with the oceanic hues of the beach and water. The wrist watch on the left wrist left no doubt.

"Do you want to say hi to my camera?" I asked.

"Hi, camera," he chuckled, looking straight at me while continuing to pedal. Behind him in full splendor, the sandy beach and baby blue ocean further glistened from the bouncing sun rays.

"*Hah, hah, hah,* what's your name?" I wasn't laughing at him. My voice had a shakiness to it from the bounce of the bike.

"John."

"Where are you from?"

He pedaled for a moment before turning his head towards me, "Do you want my social security number too?" I noticed the grin and chuckle.

"No, I don't actually. I'm from Minneapolis. I'm on a little tour."

"Oh, really. We were just in Minneapolis."

"I went to American Idol last night."

"Did you?" he said in genuine amazement.

"That's why I came to L.A."

"Who won?"

"Well, the results are tonight. That was the final performance show."

We engaged in more small talk, and appreciated our commonalities. Saying our goodbyes, we parted ways.

Pedaling back to the Santa Monica Pier, I asked the hot dog vendor again, "Do you know when he is going to open up?"

"He's inside setting up, I'll get him for you." With that he disappeared through the door to the Route 66 kiosk.

I walked over and peered in with impatience. The hot dog vendor emerged. The gentleman inside said, "Hi, I'm setting up now. Give me ten minutes."

"Ok, I can wait."

The metal slide gate on the front of the kiosk finally opened up. "Once I finish setting up, I can help you. Please be patient. It will only be a few minutes."

"No problem, I can wait."

Henry stood 5'9" tall; a twentysomthing Hispanic man dressed in a black Route 66 t-shirt and tanish shorts with tennis shoes and dark socks. Squeaky clean, he combed his hair straight back in neat fashion, and had scruff on his chin, all the while donning sunglasses.

I needed an interview, and I couldn't pass up the opportunity. He continued to multitask, setting up the kiosk and helping a few straggling customers. Inner pangs grew into anxieties, necessitating an explanation to him about the urgency of the situation.

"Just a few more minutes and I'll be ready."

"I got to get an interview," I said.

"This is a once in a lifetime thing, you have to do it," he said, relaxed and smiling.

"I know. That's how I feel. First things first. I'm either going to buy a t-shirt or buy a book, but not both."

"Not a problem, take your time." I purchased the book, *End of the Trail*, by Dan Rice.

At 11:45 am the interview began. A large blue Route 66 map marked the back of the kiosk. I said into my camera, "Hi. This is the Mr. Y. BBQ Tour. Of course I'm a Route 66 fanatic. You see behind me the map, right there," I pointed, "and I am standing right here, on the pier in Santa Monica." I pointed again. "With me here today is ... what's the name of the shop?"

"66-Cali."

"66-Cali. It's a shop right here as you come down into the pier. It's all about Route 66. If you ever come here you have to come to the shop. Now, give me your name."

"Henry, my name is Henry."

"You work here, right?"

"Absolutely."

"And you know everything there is to know about Route 66?"

"There's some bias there, but yes."

"So share with us a little bit about what you know."

Henry stood facing the camera, hands in his pockets. "To give you a brief history of Route 66, it's the first paved American highway." He pulled his left hand out and waved it in front of him like a professor does during a lecture. "It starts in Chicago and ends here at the Santa Monica Pier." He pointed to Chicago on the map, then Santa Monica. "The route builders connected every main street from every state that goes across, and paved it all the way through, making it the first paved highway in the United States." He glided his hand over the map following the red line that signified the highway.

"Thank you, Henry. High five."

"I'm excited to see how this turned out. I've never done this before," he said.

"I can assure you Henry you did great. When I finish the video, I'll send you an email." I learned more about Route 66 in those few moments with Henry than I've learned during an entire lifetime. Over time, governments built paved interstates bypassing Route 66. Angel Delgadillo fought with them to build more exits, otherwise they'd kill businesses. But governments didn't listen. One by one business after business closed. Soon government revenues were in significant decline. They went to Angel and asked what they could do. He informed them there was nothing to do as there were no more businesses to save. That is when Angel Delgadillo started the Route 66 Association in Arizona, and single-handedly saved Route 66.

Dan Rice, owner of 66-Cali and the author of *End of the Trail*, has traveled Route 66 twenty-five times. Every tourist sees, a few feet from his kiosk, a prominent sign declaring SANTA MONICA, 66, END OF THE TRAIL. We can thank him for that. It was his efforts that got the city of Santa Monica to recognize the Pier as the end of The Mother Road. Lucky for me, Dan loves barbeque, too, and here are his favorite Route 66 barbeque places, as told via email:

1. *Missouri Hick BBQ*, they've won multiple awards and are located in Cuba, Missouri.
2. *Elbow Inn BBQ*, the pulled pork is fantastic, but the sauce divine, located in Devils Elbow, Missouri.
3. *The Boundary on 66 BBQ*, their pulled pork is phenomenal (it has cheese mixed in!), tell Buffy that Dan Rice sent you, located between Chandler and Arcadia, Oklahoma, (right outside Oklahoma City).

Dan added one more tidbit: "For some people, road trips began in Detroit with the advent of the automobile, and since US 12 still runs unbroken to the beginning of Route 66 in Chicago, I'll throw one great addendum to my earlier list by including *Slows Bar BQ,* which is at the beginning of US 12 in Detroit—really fantastic."

Their infectious fire for all things Route 66 reignited my curiosity and triggered the adventurer within. I stood ready to conquer ocean and mountain alike. Being there felt like being on an episode of *the History Channel,* and having to leave drew a parallel to my teddy bear being taken away.

My problem now had to do with time. It was noon and I hadn't even returned the rental bike or checked out of the hostel yet. The Paramount Tour started at 12:30 pm. On their website they said to be there a half hour early, in this case, at noon.

Living by the seat of my pants is a common occurrence for me. My question now had to do with how to snatch victory from the jaws of defeat: "Oh, I knew it. That L.A. Traffic, I knew it. It got you. That darn L.A. Traffic. We're booked full for the rest of the day. Let me look again. Nope. All the tours are full. That L.A. Traffic. I knew it. I knew it. It got you. I'll refund your ticket," the Paramount customer service representative said over the phone. *Hah*, victory!

Wow, I thought. I slammed Paramount Studios on Facebook, and now this guy is the greatest customer service guy ever and gives me a refund. I feel so stupid. They should hire a million of him.

Fortunately for me, Warner Bros. had a 1:40 pm opening. Getting there presented its own challenges. I had been vague about writing down the directions, and driving north on 101, an ever-common Los Angeles dilemma presented itself. The highway split into two pieces, each going a different direction. Oh no, I thought.

I got their customer service guy on the phone who clarified the situation.

The Warner Bros. VIP Tour snaked through their working studio. They don't have a fancy amusement park or tourist-only attractions. Everything seen is the real deal.

The Voice films on Sound Stage 16. It's the third largest Sound Stage in the world and the largest in North America. Sound Stage 24 has a plaque honoring that *Friends* had been filmed there. Same for Sound Stage 11 for *ER*.

On TV the streets, buildings, and outdoor areas look huge, all because of the ability of the camera to fool the viewer. On one back lot the buildings are built shorter and shorter going down the street, making the road look like it goes on around the bend forever. In reality it stops right there. Building that way gives the illusion of long distances on camera. Clever.

The Smithsonian wanted the CENTRAL PERK set from *Friends* for their museum. Warner Bros. said no and now it is a stop on the tour. They own the only in-studio jungle in Hollywood and the lake used in the famous George Clooney scene in *ER*, where he tries to save a girl, can be filled or emptied in eight hours. By the way, when George shivered like he was cold, he wasn't. The water gets warmed to 85 degrees.

Speaking of George Clooney, before he made it big on *ER*, he pushed to have a gym built for workers and actors. The executives said no. George persisted. One high-up executive told him, with the wink of an eye, to get signatures from a hundred Warner Bros. executives and he would build the gym, figuring George could never do it.

George came back with one signature. The executive took one look and ordered the gym built. That one signature belonged to none other than Clint Eastwood. Nobody says no to Clint.

We visited the building housing the photo cars,

meaning any car appearing on camera. Gosh darn, it was a throwback in time all the way back to my youth. All the famous cars were in there: the Batmobile, General Lee, and even the Harry Potter car, to name a few. The Gran Torino, used in the movie *Gran Torino* still belongs to Clint. If he wants to drive it away, he can.

The famous HOLLYWOOD sign is, in the literal sense, right on the other side of the hill from the studio. Attempting to find it using the directions listed on their handout led to a wild goose chase up and down steep canyon roads.

The problem, in part, were the multiple Franklin Avenues and lack of a North Beachwood Blvd. Never one to give up and using the finer elements of persistence, I slogged through until I achieved my goal of getting a good picture of the sign. I snapped away under warm sun and blue skies, happy to be where I was.

CHAPTER 19

dip went the finger

Asking a drunk guy in a liquor store for directions to downtown Los Angeles is never a good idea. He slobbered, got demanding, and slurred his speech so bad I thought he might be speaking Chinese, even though he was white Anglo-Saxon. I used boundary skills I learned at the school to tell him to stay put and not come an inch closer, then I hopped in the car and burned rubber out of there.

It took me two hours to drive the eight miles to the Nokia Theater Plaza. I didn't let the traffic jams bother me too much. I saw it as an opportunity to soak up every last sunny moment, since my plane left for Minneapolis later that night.

So far on this trip, despite good intentions, there had been no barbeque. Stuff kept getting in the way, and the fact that barbeque wasn't a priority didn't make it any easier.

I strolled into Nokia Plaza like everyone else awaiting the American Idol Finale results. I felt a mixture of curiosity and a good kind of mild anxiety. I had voted for Jessica Sanchez, but if Phillip Phillips won, then more power to him. I still thought his song, *Home,* was the knockout blow. Mulling around I got a burst of boldness. I swung around to a security guard full of grit and asked, "Are there any good barbeque places around here?"

"Sure. ESPN has some good barbeque. On the other side of the block, on the next street over, is Trader Vic's. They're really good." He emphasized Trader Vic's by a large margin. Since this would be the only barbeque on the entire trip I didn't waste a single solitary second and made a bee-line over there.

They had all the markings of a chain. The wood-grained surfboard above the bar dining room read, TRADER VIC'S LOS ANGELES, giving them away. They helped pioneer the introduction of PuPu cuisine to North America from Hawaii during a time when society really craved Polynesian food in the style of the 1940s and 1950s.

Bamboo fixtures dotted the interior and Polynesian designs decorated the walls. Tribal light shades and masks gave it a finishing touch. The tables and bar were made from heavy wood, probably bamboo, smooth and lacquered to the hilt.

I had seen those designs, masks, and light shades before when I traveled to Indonesia. Trader Vic's could be Polynesian, or Indonesian, or Hawaiian, or even Filipino. Hawaii used to have a Filipino king and people have migrated between Indonesia and the Philippines for ages. The first scan of the menu didn't yield barbeque. The closest item was BBQ VEGETABLES & TOFU.

"Excuse me, do you serve any sort of barbeque ribs here? Someone said you did," I said to the hostess manning the cash register in the main hallway.

"Yes, it's right here." She pointed to BBQ PORK SPARERIBS, listed under the TIDBITS AND PUPS section.

"Oh, thank you. I didn't see it before. I'll take that to go."

"Sure, no problem. Would you like to wait in the bar area?"

"Yes."

Sitting there, a waiter brought me a cool refreshing glass of ice water. After a couple of sips I developed a need to visit the restroom, leaving the glass on the table until I got back. A few minutes later, when I arrived back, it went missing. Boy they're quick, I thought.

Plucking up to the bar I said, "Excuse me, could I have another glass of water?" I took some sips from the new glass of water, but again I developed a need to visit the restroom. I came back in less than a minute, and my glass of water went missing, again.

What is this, I thought, pissed. Trader Vic's 2, Mr. Y. 0. Saving the day, the hostess showed up with the ribs. Lucky for them. *Grrrrr, take my glass one more time ....*

The growl in my stomach increased to a point of desperation. The aroma of the ribs proved unbearable. I carried the plastic container containing the ribs back to the Plaza—I didn't want to miss the announcement of the Idol winner—and found a nice looking stone bench kitty corner from Wolfgang Puck. I ripped the cover off and peered in. Joy got into a tug of war with disappointment.

Glistening in the bright sun were five, browned-just-enough, delicious-looking ribs. In one corner, like in a boxing match, sat a small container of mustard sauce. In the other corner, a small container of red sauce.

I searched the four corners of the plastic container for sides. I looked on top of and underneath the ribs too. None were found. Sides, there were no all-important sides.

I gripped the first bone and dipped it with arrogance into the mustard sauce, then took a big bite. Somebody, somewhere, call the fire department. The Marine Corps. has a philosophy that says, *Don't believe anything you hear and only half of what you see.* In my ignorance I believed everything I saw. Besides, that mustard sauce looked like honey mustard, how hot can it be? And for all who heard the yelps shooting from my mouth from the burning fire in there, believe what you heard!

I didn't believe what the tongue felt, so I drove the bone down again, driving it deep into the mustard sauce.

Same insane result. This time my brain acknowledged the senses getting torched.

Dip went my finger into the red sauce. Then I touched my tongue. Safe. Bland. I tried again, hoping for a different result. Nope. Safe. Bland.

Red sauces are typically in one camp or the other; tangy or sweet. This sauce tasted strangely familiar. I poured it all over bone, and took another bite. Same result. Safe. Bland. I racked my brain because the sauce tasted familiar ... mmmm ... pizza! That's it! It tasted like the tomato sauce used on pizza.

I didn't dare try the mustard sauce again, but I did slather on more red sauce. I ran out of sauce, leaving a couple of bones dry. I ripped through them faster than normal because I didn't have any sides to slow me down.

The ribs were cooked to a nice color brown and the meat looked tender. In reality, though, the ribs were like the red sauce. Great looking, but safe, bland. The meat didn't slide off, but I didn't have to rip it off either. It came off easy, but work was needed and they were on the dry side, too.

All in all my rib eating experience at Trader Vic's could be summarized as a little bit of joy, a bigger glob of disappointment, with safe and bland added in heavy doses.

I couldn't blame Trader Vic's for this. They are Polynesian or Indonesian or Hawaiian or Filipino, take your pick. Barbeque isn't their specialty. The lack of sides says it all. California doesn't know barbeque like Kentucky or Tennessee; the Champions of Barbeque. They can't be faulted. If I went up against Muhammad Ali in his prime, I'd go down in defeat, too. That's the plain reality; *Noth'n but the truth my friend, noth'n but the truth.*

Idol fans mulled around the press area. Earlier, the security guard had made it plain no one would be allowed near. However, individual black metal railings were still stacked in piles throughout the plaza and no security guards were in sight. No one came up to me and said, "Please move it along, sir."

I searched for the perfect place to stand. It took keen investigation of every inch. Multiple factors came into play. On the far corner of the press area, closest to Staples Center, stood a short, cute Japanese girl with her parents. A super duper camera dangled from her hand. I found the perfect spot.

The crowd kept forming and the party expanding. "Who are you rooting for?" I asked to no one in particular, attempting to make small talk.

"Phillip Phillips."

"Oh, I'm rooting for Jessica," I said.

45 minutes, at the latest, would be my drop dead time to head for the airport. The crowd roared like a deprived tiger, the bodies kept coming and coming, cramming the fence—like sardines.

First I heard a dull roar which turned into applause. Then it changed to screams and high pitched cheers. Those nearby stayed glued to their Smartphones, possessed. Pandemonium erupted.

"Who won?" I asked a girl on the other side of me.

"PHILLIP PHILLIPS!!!" Screams, more screams.

Squished to the fence the short Japanese girl stood next to me, elbow to elbow. "Who are you rooting for?" I asked.

"I rooted for Jeremy," making no attempt to hide her enthusiasm. Jeremy stood a few feet away, interviewed by a reporter looking for the next big story.

Soon, the Top 12 Idol contestants appeared. Not Phillip or Jessica, though. I found myself smooshed against the fence with nowhere or way to move. My camera ran out of power. Two days in a row now. I learned to shut it off for a few minutes and then turn it back on. This did the trick as it had enough power to snap still photos. Shannon, DeAndre, Hejun, Colton, Elise, Hollie and Skylar. I got them all.

Idol contestants have earned the utmost in respect. They are pushed, pulled, and poked from all sides by handlers, reporters, friends, fans, whomever. Fans battle inches away for a picture or autograph. Kids scream, moms yell, dads scoff.

The weak spot in our human existence is on full display. Competitiveness and selfishness reach new heights while forgiveness and *I'm sorry* are sent to the trash can. Through it all, Idol contestants maintain their poise and humility. Hooray for them; I stand in awe.

"Oh, Hejun, I love you, I love you. You're the best. Are you making an album? You should have your own show. You are so funny. You are so funny!" the youthful-mannered woman said, screaming at the top of her lungs inches from my ear. She pushed and shoved, "Oh, Hejun, can I have your autograph, please? Can I have your autograph, please? I love you. I love you." She squealed louder and louder, a few decibels short of breaking my eardrum. Hejun obliged. "I love you! I love you!" she screamed, that elderly woman, louder and louder.

When contestants are hauled away by their handlers as though under arrest, they feel bad, saying, "I'll come back," followed by a smile and a wave. The fans don't hide their disappointment, making sad faces and whispering in dejection while turning away. It's rare the Idol ever returns, though not of their own doing.

Shannon, voted off contestant number 11, answered questions from the interviewer with grace and charm. Decked out in a beautiful dress, she accommodated the demands of an Idol contestant like a pro. "Jennifer's something else isn't she? She really knows how to pop it," she said referring to Jennifer Lopez.

The reporter interviewing her had buzzed around the press area with the instincts of a stealth fighter for the last two days. Intuition says he worked for a local Los Angeles TV station. Mid-forties, decked out in a dark blue sport coat, no tie, looking like a 6'2" version of Tom

Cruise, or better yet a huskier version of Matthew Mc-Conaughey or even Channing Tatum.

Possessing a stud persona, if he wasn't a reporter he would be an actor, replete with being a Ladies Man. When he flashed his Hollywood smile the whites of his teeth glowed in the afternoon sun. His Hollywood hair-style looked expensive. Close-cropped, almost military like, it increased in thickness ending in a full head of hair at the top. Parted on the left, combed to the right, it ended in a hook reminiscent of Clark Kent.

The charm and sexiness which he possessed were on full display when he interviewed Shannon. He treated her with complete professionalism, like the veteran reporter he was.

Off camera he said to her, "Thanks for doing the interview." Pausing, standing tall, the glare of the lights behind him, flashing that broad Hollywood smile, he added, "You look stunningly gorgeous tonight," stretching the word *stunningly*, and breathing *gorgeous* with sharp baritone richness. Imagine the sexiest man alive saying this at the peak of romance to Catherine Zeta-Jones in the most romantic movie ever made.

The short Japanese girl, still next to me, couldn't see above the bodies in front of her. Up went her arm, *click*. Moving it left, *click*. Moving it right, *click*. Pointing it up, *click*. Pointing it down, *click*. In between clicks the crowd stampeded forward squishing her like a pancake. Her face jammed into the middle of the back of the person in front of her, becoming contorted in a painful way.

"It must be hard getting pictures when you can't see above the crowd?" I said.

She tilted her head towards me in a slight way, still smiling. "Yes." Her body twisted in three different directions.

"Does your camera only take still pictures, or does it do video too?"

Smiling again, "Only stills." Up went her arm, *click*.

Moving it left, *click*. Moving it right, *click*. Pointing it up, *click*. Pointing it down, *click*.

Dang. We would make the cutest couple ever, I thought.

The time on my cell phone said 7:45 pm, and it was time to go. I pushed through the screaming mass of humanity. The party showed no signs of slowing down anytime soon.

"How do I get to the airport from here?" I asked the policeman in the alleyway.

"Where are you parked?"

"Firgusa, Figusia, something like that," I said, butchering the street name. I took a moment to regain my composure. I pointed in the direction of the parking lot, "It's a few blocks away."

"Take this street to 110 south, then take 105 west. Be sure to take 105 west," the policeman said, pointing to the street in front of us.

I have plenty of time, I thought, ever the optimist. Following what the policeman said, but missing the 105 west cutoff after enacting heroic driving maneuvers, I stared down stoplights at an intersection in an unfamiliar area. The kind employees at a nearby McDonald's pointed me the right way to the airport.

Crap, I only have 45 minutes before my flight takes off. I don't know where to unload. I'm not even close to checking in. I might miss my flight. How come there's so much traffic? It seems like every hour is rush hour in Los Angeles. Is everybody leaving L.A. at the same time? How come a cement truck is driving around LAX this time of night?

There are two kinds of signs at LAX. One is for returning a rental car, listed as P1 or P2 or P3 depending on which car rental outfit is used. The other kind says 1 or 2 or 3 and so on, depending on which airline is needed. Underneath 1, for example, it listed a whole bunch of airlines with a sign underneath that says NEXT TERMINAL, with arrows pointing forward.

US Airways is at the next Terminal, I thought. The big numbers on the big pillars kept incrementing. First 1, then 2, then 3, and so on. More heroic maneuvers and a switch in lanes resulted in being stuck behind a cement truck, city bus, car, car, car, and an RV.

Another heroic lane switch landed me at a red light. There are more stoplights at LAX alone than your average big city downtown. The light turned green and I made more progress, but soon found myself stopped at another red light. The big number on the big pillar said 6. How many Terminals do they have, I wondered, now near panic.

Wait. I figured out the signs! The first sign when I entered LAX had a big 1 in the upper left corner. It listed a number of airlines, followed by NEXT TERMINAL at the bottom. What it means is I am at Terminal 1 and those are the airlines for Terminal 1. The NEXT TERMINAL is just pointing the way to the next Terminal, meaning Terminal 2. It doesn't mean those airlines are at Terminal 2, it means keep going ahead for the next Terminal. Darn it.

I made countless loops before discovering the RETURN TO TERMINAL lane. I can't begin to describe the sense of relief I felt.

Once I found the unloading area I gathered my things and ran into the Terminal full speed (don't even ask about the rental car). I asked the nearest employee, "Where is the check-in for US Airways?" I barely had the breath to finish the question.

"Upstairs and to the left, sir."

Both the ticket and security check-ins went smoothly, 20 minutes before liftoff. The tension in my shoulders lifted. My breathing slowed, and I walked with a calm swagger to the gate, as though nothing had happened. *Phew!*

CHAPTER 20

henry knows

I burst through the doors on that Friday afternoon. Finding him hunched over piles of camping saws, I couldn't wait to talk to him. On this blistering hot sunny day he wore a long sleeve shirt, like always.

"Hey Henry, how are you?" (No relation to Henry on the Santa Monica Pier).

"Good, how about yourself?"

"Great, I just got back from Los Angeles yesterday."

"Los Angeles?" Surprise attacked his face, invading his voice, too. A year ago he uprooted his family from there and on more than one occasion let me know how he missed the weather.

"Yes, it was great. I ate barbeque there too. I went on a barbeque tour last summer and made some YouTube videos out of them. I figured since I was out in L.A. I might as well make it part of my tour. Have you ever heard of a place called Trader Vic's?"

He strolled to the back of the work area, "No."

"Well, I went to Trader Vic's and tried their barbeque ribs and they weren't very good. No sides."

Henry looked up from the bench. "No sides?" He sounded like an echo. His quiet, unassuming nature offered no clues to his violent, gang-infested past.

We've had the most liberating discussions. I learned he got sentenced to prison for killing a man, a year for each bullet in his gun; 12 to be exact. It's there, in prison, where he experienced a religious conversion.

I discovered why he always wore long sleeve shirts;

It's to cover the tattoos. My curiosity on why he uprooted his family to Chaska on a dime got answered; his internet research said it was the best place to live in the United States.

Continuing with my diatribe, "They had this mustard sauce that lit my mouth on fire and this red sauce that tasted like tomato paste for pizza," gritting my teeth, not able to contain my resentment over the red sauce.

"That's terrible." He sorted through more camping saws, looking for mistakes.

"It *was* terrible."

He looked up from the pile and spoke in a discerning Hispanic accent, "That's a bummer, you really missed out."

"I know. It sucks. I found out about a place in Redondo Beach called Pinkies. It's supposed to be world-famous, but I didn't make it there. The Promenade in Santa Monica near where I stayed had like six barbeque places. I missed all of those, too."

He smiled at this. "Oh man, there's barbeque all over. Pinkies is famous. It's good, but it's not the best." Living in Los Angeles his whole life up, close to half a century, he would know.

Looking straight at him, I asked "What place do you like? Where do you think the best place is?" I needed to know what he knew.

Without hesitation he answered, "Man, if you want the best, go to Lucille's."

"Where's that?"

"There's *two* of them. One near Disneyland in Anaheim and the other near Pasadena. There's nothing that compares to Lucille's. It's the best."

"Oh man, I blew it." Henry knows.

CHAPTER 21

do it now

I went in search of the perfect barbeque. I am convinced I'll be on this search the rest of my life. It simply will not end. The reason is easy to figure out: everybody has their own opinion and their own taste. When it comes to barbeque, everyone has an ego the size of the sun. For each, theirs is the best and there is no other. They know of a little barbeque place just off the road, somewhere, that just can't be beat.

Secret rubs and secret sauces, loaded with secret ingredients, are applied in the most secretive of ways; a family relative, cloaked in a shroud of secrecy, smokes the barbeque immersed in exotic woods no one ever thought of. That's part of the fun!

Whenever I mentioned to someone I'm on a barbeque tour *something* sparked. Perhaps a burst of energy triggered or a competitiveness went on high alert or an ego unhinged itself. Whatever it was it came out, took over, and dominated the conversation.

It's unassailable that it was all in good fun. No one ever wished any harm or had mean thoughts of destruction upon their fellow man who may not agree with them—they just think their barbeque is better. The lady at Famous Dave's brought home this point. Oh, yes, I talked to her too. She dreamed of going to St. Louis to eat ribs. I know just the place.

But being in search for the perfect barbeque was but a small part—very small part. At every place I visited I always came out the winner. I love ribs and I love eating.

McCoy and Sandifer can attest to that. I am the Champ! I like sweet more than spicy. I like baked beans and I like applesauce. I like Memphis-style ribs, St. Louis-style ribs, Kansas City-style ribs, and Arkansas-style ribs. Heck, I like them all. What I liked most, though, are the stories. The Americana. Every person, every town, every maker of barbeque had a story to tell, and they shared those stories with me. That was the crux, the purpose, the hidden jewels of my tour. I lived the family traditions, egos, competition, values, friendliness, adventures, and fun.

Now, those stories are waiting for you. It doesn't matter whether you are in Louisville or Chicago or Springfield or St. Louis or Kansas City or St. Paul or Los Angeles or Minneapolis or St. Paul or Elgin or Atlanta or Longmont or Plant City. They are waiting. All you have to do is listen. That, my friends, is the beauty. America, for that matter the World, is waiting to touch your ears. Listen. I dare you. Do it now.

The Fever can't but you can! Be ready. Life throws us curveballs. Go to some stranger, someone not far from you, and ask him or her about barbeque. Do it now. Do it for yourself. Do it for The Fever. Listen, just listen.

Something will spark, trigger if you will. They will share their life. They will persuade you they make the best barbeque on the planet, or have an uncle or a brother that does. Something about their sauce and the wood they use and their special way of cooking them. They will tell you about this little mom and pop place in the middle of Podunk, Nowheresville, that has been there a 100 years, and their barbeque can't be beat.

It won't matter what state of affairs their life is in. Eyes will light up, smiles will explode, and a fire will jump from their belly when they tell you their story. Friends are made forever. Ask. I dare you. Then listen. That's all you have to do. Please, for The Fever's sake, do it now.

* * *

In a final note, lightning struck the house I live in. It started a blistering, nervous fire in the garage, sending billowing smoke from all corners of our residence. Seven fire trucks and three squad cars arrived to put the darn thing out. We made the 5 o'clock news.

Thank goodness no one was hurt, but as a consequence, all of us living there, my dad, me, two siblings, two cats, and Milo the dog became refugees vacated to a local Inn. We did the best circumstances would allow. We were ordered to take essential belongings with us, of which we complied. Naturally, I grabbed The Fever.

After four weeks we were ordered back into the house, as after much work, it was now semi-livable. Two nights after returning family chaos erupted. It started back at the Inn and carried over. A car went missing, a person disappeared, slurred speech entered the picture, a homeless person hid in the closet, cats pooped everywhere, a search team scoured the streets, and the police were involved. All told, emotions were raw. All traced, BTW, to a single drink of alcohol. To add to this, the furnace got red-tagged and the house went cold—in 20 below weather.

The garage structure still needs replacing after which the entire roof is to be re-shingled. Meanwhile contractors are showing up to finish off a laundry list of work: sand floors, install the electrical box and circuit breakers, restore phone and internet service, clean walls, and so on.

I lay in bed one night wide awake at 3 am, ruminating about all of this. I remained conflicted in my emotions, knowing that serious decisions had to be made. Somehow, in the midst of this chaos, a single thought burst from the empty darkness. I left him, The Fever, in his little silver container, in a cabinet high

above the refrigerator at the Inn. Now, it's a Rescue
Operation.

THE END

acknowledgments

I want to thank my editors Rebecca Justiniano, Delores Topliff, and Ghazal Ghazi, whose job it was to keep me in line! I want to thank, too, my brothers Pete and Greg for putting up with me. And I can't leave out Lisa Ocone, whose persistent encouragement got me started. I'm grateful to Ann Rodning for her insightful comments and to Tim Johnson for dreaming up the cover concept. I humbly thank all whom I met in my journeys and were gracious enough to talk to me.

references

1. Chapter 1, 2011, Definition of Tangent, (http://www.thefreedictionary.com/tangent)

2. Chapter 5, 2011, St. Louis Arch, (http://en.wikipedia.org/wiki/Gateway_Arch)

3. Chapter 5, 2010, Target Field, Jim Souhan, Earl Santee: He Built It, (http://www.startribune.com/templates/Print_This_Story?sid=112415774)

4. Chapter 6, 2011, Definition of Burnt Ends, http://pelletenvy.blogspot.com/2008/02/burnt-ends.html)

5. Chapter 6, 2012, Hawaiian PuPu Cuisine, (http://www.ohanarecipes.com/recipes_pupus.htm)

6. Chapter 6, 2012, Eclipse Chasers Look to Kentucky, (http://www.sci-tech-today.com/news/Eclipse-Chasers-Look-to-Kentucky-/story.xhtml?story_id=00200042K9H2)

7. Chapter 9, 2011, (http://www.owensboro.org/about/owensboro)

8. Chapter 9, 2011, Roy Henry, (http://www.boogaloubbq.com)

9. Chapter 19, 2015, Dan Harkins, What is a PuPu Platter?, (http://www.wisegeek.com/what-is-a-pu-pu-platter.htm)

trailer

During the summer the school day at the correctional facility where I work ends at noon. On this particular Monday a hand waved me over on the way out of the lunchroom. Action Jackson wanted my presence. Plopping down next to him, he had on a nice blue polo shirt and light colored dress pants.

Head tilted down, peering over his glasses, he said, "Have you had barbeque lately?"

"Not lately. Well, I did try some on my trip to Los Angeles a few weeks ago. Some Polynesian place. The ribs looked good. But the mustard sauce lit my mouth on fire and the red sauce tasted like tomato paste for pizza."

He nodded, "That's typical." Still staring over the top of his glasses, "I've been working on my barbeque. I just made some. Has anyone ever used paprika?"

"No, I've never heard of anyone using that."

"I use paprika and garlic and ...." I lost track of all the things he used. By now his eyes were shooting over the rim of his glasses like laser beams. He faced me square. "I wrap it in tin foil and poke holes in a circle, then I place it by the coals, then I move it, then I place it by the wood, then I move it again. It's awesome. I'm really getting it." While saying this he simulated the wrapping of ribs in foil followed by the poking of holes in it by a fork. He finished by moving the imaginary ribs to different places on the lunch table.

Curiosity entered the picture. I said, "How do you rate compared to your brother's?"

"I'm at the bottom of the totem pole," he said as he

began rattling off the names of his brothers in rapid succession.

"I mean the one you were talking about before, the one in California who makes barbeque."

"I'm way down at the bottom. He's Wolfgang Puck and I'm starting out. How do you compare?" his voice trailing. After a brief pause he recharged. "I never use lighter fluid. Ever. I use one of those chimney smokes. You wouldn't even have to taste the smokiness. You would just pick it up and go, 'Umm, smokey.' I've figured out that when they use those bigger smokers, it makes the ribs a lot more smokey."

"It probably surrounds the ribs from all directions," I said.

"Yep."

"You know I'm gonna want some."

"If I brought in even a sample you would say, 'That's it. Over. Done.'"

A few weeks later I sat at the computer with mouse in hand. I was getting ready to make the move of the century. I am going to get him, I thought, wait until he sees *this* move. Checkmate! You're finished, buddy.

Then I heard him, my dad. "Tim, Tim, TIIIIIIIM-MMM!," he yelled from the living room, clear on the other side of the house.

I jumped up and stomped down the hallway. "*WHAAAAAT*? What do you want?" I said, knowing he heard the irritation in my voice. I didn't try to disguise it.

"It's Pete, he's on the phone."

Still irritated I snapped the phone from his hand. "Yeah?!" I said into it while stomping back down the hall.

"Yeah, man. Me and Pete went to this barbeque place in Chicago. Smoque or something like that. We took pictures and shot some video. We interviewed the owner. The barbeque was really great man," Greg said.

Feeling his excitement through the phone, but struggling to understand the words because he talked so fast, I said, "Really? Was it good?" The bitterness I felt for my chess game being interrupted subsided.

"Yeah man, it was great. Pete really liked it."

"Is it better than I-57 BBQ?"

"Yeah man, it's like ten times better than I-57. Pete said it's one of the best barbeques he's ever had. It was great. We got pictures and video. We'll show them to you when we get back."

"Hey thanks, cool. Yeah, show it to me when you get back." By now the guilt for snapping at my dad had me on my emotional knees.